MYSTIC Fathers

KEVIN ERNEST HALL

Introduction into
12 mystical men
from the Monastic Era

Published by Seraph Creative

Mystic Fathers
Copyright© 2020 by Kevin Ernest Hall

All rights reserved. This book is protected by the USA, UK and international copyright laws. This book may not be copied or reprinted for commercial gain or profit. The use of short quotations or occasional page copying for personal or group study is permitted and encouraged. Permission will be granted upon request.

Published by Seraph Creative in 2020
United States / United Kingdom / South Africa / Australia
www.seraphcreative.org

Typesetting & Layout by Feline
www.felinegraphics.com

Printed in USA, UK and RSA, 2020

All rights reserved. No part of this book, artwork included, may be used or reproduced in any matter without the written permission of the publisher.

Print ISBN 978-1-922428-10-3
eBook ISBN 978-1-922428-11-0

"Almighty God, unto whom all hearts are open, all desires known, and from whom no secrets are hid; cleanse the thoughts of our hearts by the inspiration of your Holy Spirit, that we may perfectly love you, and worthily magnify your holy name, through Christ, our Lord."

John Chrysostom

I dedicate this book to my boys, Nathan and Ryan Hall, they gave me the gift of entering into our lives and learning how to be their dad. What a journey this has been, moments of great joy, many tears.

Moments filled with insects and lizards, dirty pants, climbing trees, boys are boys, and in this process, I learned about the Love of God towards His sons. I dedicate this book to the boys, guys I love you more than words on a page could ever describe, I thought I knew love, until I met you both, thank you for just being crazy and fun. I love you so very much and trust you will give me the grace and mercy to learn how to be a better dad.

Foreword

Once upon a time, I had only been the keynote speaker at a conference one other time, I was not married, I had only sold a few copies of my books and I only had a few dollars to my name. What I did have was a good attitude, a great friend named Chris and a meeting with some guy named Kevin who my friend Chris said loved Jesus and could open some doors. Today I average fifteen countries a year, have more than a few dollars, am married to my dream come true and have a group of people across the world that love and walk with me. It is expanding at a rate I do not understand. The meeting with Kevin Hall that Chris took me too was the connection point for the relationships and the catalyst for everything I mentioned above, including meeting my future wife the same day I met Kevin. He introduced us.

Now, many years later he has taken me on some of the wildest adventures I have ever been on, been with me during some of the funniest experiences I have ever had and shown me some of the most special and holy places I have ever been to. He has introduced me to mentors, taken me on safaris and driven me to churches and venues in some of the most remote places in the world so that we could "preach the good news." In doing all of that, much of which was at his own expense, the only thing he has ever asked me to do for him is write a foreword to his book. This is the quality of person whose book you have chosen to read. Without exception, no matter what comes our way I will love and trust him forever, he is my brother and friend.

Kevin is also uniquely qualified to write a book about the mystic fathers. First, Kevin has studied and done the legwork in research to bring a picture of them and who they were as accurately as possible. He has done real research and moved beyond today's self-proclaimed expert research phenomenon, Wikipedia. It is evident in his writing. Second, Kevin is a mystic himself. In my sometimes-humble opinion if you are going to write a book about mystics you should have at the very least a little bit of mystical experience and understanding in your life. Kevin has it. Two weeks before I wrote this draft I was traveling to Texas and he sent me a text not knowing what I was doing and began to describe some of the elements that would be involved in the trip that I was already engaging. It moved into the mystical aspects of what was happening with the knowledge that someone who is not a mystic could not have otherwise. Kevin "does the work" consistently and unselfishly for the benefit of those around him. He prays and engages around others more than most do for themselves and in the four nations I have been with him in Kevin does his best to honor the culture in a way that would actually honor them. The reason this applies to the book is it is possible to insert your own ideals into someone's life you are writing about and it takes a measure of objectivity to both communicate what you want to communicate and hold the integrity of what their lives actually demonstrated. It is a monumentally difficult task for an author and Kevin has done it well in this piece.

I am of the firm belief that if we are to understand where we are going, we need to fully grasp our roots. While the reader may have never heard of some of these fathers, they are all markers in history to look back upon, learn from and remember. We would not be where were are today without all of them. Many of the things we as mystics see as common place are because of the battles these men have fought. Sadly, the measure of glory all of these men walked in far surpasses what we experience today and maybe, just maybe, in having an objective window opened to us we could look back upon their lives, learn something and grow into a fuller expression of what YHVH wants to express on The Earth in our day. May you be abundantly enlightened, illuminated, provoked, driven and motivated through Kevin's hard work and the lives of The Mystic Fathers.

Deep Love,

Joseph C Sturgeon II

Acknowledgements

Thank you, Abba Father, for teaching me your ways, for showing me your love, and for displaying your mercy to me.

To Carike Hall, my wife, thank you so much for loving me the way you do, all the hours of editing, moments of helping me make sense of my words and my ideas, and turning my roughhewn thoughts into recognizable works of art.

To Dr Adonijah Ogbonnaya, as Theologian and spiritual father, thank you for all your support and your advice. Your mentorship has changed the very course and trajectory of my life.

To Joseph and Claire Sturgeon, thank you for being true friends, and showing me the face of God in real life, having people like you in my life is truly humbling.

To Chris Blackeby and Linda Lurie being my publishers, I appreciate your views, and the hard work of your team, thank you so much for helping me along this journey.

To My family and all the friends over the world, I could not mention you all by name, I appreciate you, your care, your values, and who you are helping me to become, thank you for doing life with me. I am the summary of my friends; the community of your love towards me, helps me to learn to fly into the future.

Introduction

I write this book as a pretext to understanding that the mystical view of Christianity is not just an exciting development in the Christianity of our modern times; it is a vital outflow of our epoch.

To quote the well-known catholic theologian and writer Karl Rahner: *"The Christian of the future will be a mystic or he will not exist at all."*

Having built a relationship with the mystics of the ages, during the past few years, I have encountered them from time to time in my spiritual walk. Their advice, lessons and understanding have brought me much joy, and as men of the ages, their words became like highways, bringing me closer to the eternal light of God.

This book will cover some of the seven major schools of Catholic spiritual development:

- Dessert Fathers — 3rd to 5th Century
  (Egypt / Syrian Desert)
- Monastic — 5th Century
  (Benedict and Scholastic)
- Mendicant — 13th Century
  (Frances, Dominic, St Claire of Assisi)
- Carmelite — 13th Century
  (John of the Cross; The Rule of St Albert)
- Ignatian — 16th Century
  (Ignatius Loyola)
- Salesian — 17th Century
  (Frances de Sales, Jane Frances de Chantal)
- Vincentian — 17th Century
  (St Vincent de Paul, Louise de Marillac)

Some of the schools have been excluded, due to the scope of this book focusing on the selected Saints and not to cover each school of thought. However, I tried to give a broad overview of the mystics of these schools. I also included men outside of the Catholic tradition, as I believe the church is moving away from the strict denominational divides of the past.

My relationship with each of the men in this book is very different, they all have their own way of expressing ideas, they all have their own preferences, accentuations, and areas where they would like to focus the Christian eyes and gaze of the heart. One thing remains steadfast, their lives, their eyes and their hearts are fully focused on Christ Jesus.

As mystics, they believe they can speak to God, encounter His divine voice, and have a personal relationship with the Godhead, these ideas have been very controversial throughout the ages.

Outrageous claims, unlearned men, and women, speaking directly to God, yet this is the very nature of the good news of Jesus, we can know this God, the God of the Bible. We do not need a priest, a pastor, or some initiated tribe, to teach us the ways of God, we can learn from Him directly.

Does this mean the humble men and teachers around us have no place, surely not – their roles might change, as facilitators of the divine grace, they guide us into the pathways of wisdom and help us find our own way. Yet they teach us this profound truth, Paul wrote, *"Follow me, as I follow Christ"*, insinuating that others will soon follow you, as you also follow Christ.

What do we mean by Monastic spirituality?

- Opus Dei: the purpose of monastic life is to seek God; the work of God is central to lifestyle.
- Monastic Obedience
- Monastic Silence
- Moderation
- Lectio Divina — Reading of the divine Word, while meditating on scripture
- Monastic Peace

The goal of this book is to simply introduce you to some of the mystic fathers, not an exhaustive study of their lives, thoughts, and ideas.

You might ask, how did you choose these men; well in some cases they chose me, in other situations I sort of bumped into them without planning the meeting, and in others I just saw the testimony of their lives and resonated with what they wanted to teach the earth at their different times of life.

I would encourage you, read their works, read their words, and ask the

Father of Lights to reveal their words to you, to turn their sentences into fire, burning in your heart, words aflame with love. Let the testimony of Jesus speak through their lives and make you even more hungry to spend time with the Beloved.

Then go and study, read all the commentary on their theology, understand all the nuance in their words, and like many Christians have found throughout the ages, let the mystic fathers become sages in your path to the divine relationship.

INDEX

5	Foreword
8	Acknowledgements
9	Introduction
14	Cultural and Historical context
17	Timeline
18	Chapter 1 - Benedict of Nursia
36	Chapter 2 - Francis of Assisi
50	Chapter 3 - Ignatius Loyola
62	Chapter 4 - Ivan Rilski of Rila (Bulgaria)
70	Chapter 5 - John of the Cross
82	Chapter 6 - Saint Dominic
107	Chapter 7 - Seraphim Sarov
116	Chapter 8 - Bernard of Clairvaux
126	Chapter 9 - John Van Ruysbroeck
144	Chapter 10 - Francis de Sales
158	Chapter 11 - Patrick of Ireland
168	Chapter 12 - Meister Eckhart
178	Bonus Chapter - Tekle Haymanot (Ethiopic Saint)
190	Mystical Fathers Worth Reading
191	Translations
192	Bibliography
195	Image Credits
197	About the Author
203	About Seraph Creative

Background of the "Dark Ages"

When talking about the monastic era, we need to be sensitive to the historical context these men find themselves in, and what their daily lives entailed.

The men chosen in this book, don't all have the same period of history in common, some of them lived earlier in the history of Christianity, however most of them find themselves in the "Dark Ages" or the "Middle Ages" as described by history.

Some men chosen share the same European conditions, although there are also those who don't come from continental Europe, so their understanding of the world, their experience of the world is sometimes drastically different, and the viewpoint they observe.

Abba has also allowed me to choose some men who are not all based on the same dogmatic beliefs or the same church background. I believe the diversity of the men gives the ideas in this book more strength, it is easy to see how God has spoken to a diverse group of Christian men, about the same topics, in a unique way, expressing truth in their era, their way.

The Dark Ages, a time that was literary quite dark, there was no electricity discovered, so everything that needed to be done in the evening was to be done, under the light of fires or candles.

The flickering candle was at the center of these experiences. If you wanted to read the great church fathers of years before, you would need to do so in the low light, as the dancing flame illuminated your thoughts about God.

Many monasteries became the center of learning, and the monastic communities became a place where the thoughts and ideas of the age were discussed, this only happened here, and of course in the Royal courts. The "layperson" had no access to books, reading or learning, the society operated based on agriculture and hard work and thus had to rely on the monasteries to provide insight into their faith.

The age of chivalry was alive and well, travel was made possible by horse and drawn carts, life was slow, the rhythm of life was a slow trot, sometimes things would get rowdy, the life would come to a galloping pace, where fighting or political feuds would brew, but mostly a jaunt would be the pace of most conversations, and most of the news or gossip.

The printing press was not discovered yet, so all writing was done manually, if you wanted a copy of a book, you would need to painstakingly write every word, copy the whole book, page for page. The news was not something you would buy from a news stand, or download on your iPhone, you needed to hear the news in the wind, and the gossip of the town would be the news of the day.

In this milieu, our mystics find their path, explore lofty thoughts and philosophy and delve into the depths of their Bibles, trying to pull out the truth they knew was hidden somewhere in the pages.

They would try to plumb the depths of their confessors, their spiritual directors, and any thought leaders in the old copied manuscripts to find someplace where they could find the passion, the fire burning in their hearts and minds for a God they seemed to hardly know reflected.

As we join their search and see some of the old ways of thinking, let's give them the grace and honor they deserve, we might not share their ideas, or their thoughts on God, but we definitely share their burning fire and passion for God, we share their pursuit, and we share their path, the path of the mystic, the path of mystery, where clues are few, experience is paid for in blood and sweat, and ideas can change the world we live in forever.

It is important to note, not all the mystics I chose in this book lived in this period, I have chosen some pre-monastic mystics, to show the flow of the divine revelation from one generation to the next, I have also chosen a few modern mystics, those who share our own era of about 1800, to show that the torch of mysticism has not faded into history, but is still burning bright.

I have chosen not to include those who share the 19th and 20th Century, as I believe I have already excluded enough men who should have been included but have been omitted for reasons of limited space and time in this book. Our modern age demands short and sweet, quite the opposite of the monastics and mystics who believed the ebb and flow of time would provide ample opportunity for discussion.

Timeline

	400	500	600	700	800	900	1000	1100	1200	1300	1400	1500	1600	1700	1800	1900
		Benedict of Nursia				Ivan Rilski of Rila		Bernard of Clairvaux	Saint Dominic	Francis of Assisi	John van Ruysbroeck		Ignatius Loyola	Francis de Sales / John of the Cross		Seraphim Sarov	

	John van Ruysbroeck	1293 - 1381
	Benedict of Nursia	480 - 543
	Ivan Rilski of Rila (Bulgaria)	876 - 946
	Bernard of Clairvaux	1090 - 1153
	Saint Dominic	1170 - 1221
	Francis of Assisi	1181 - 1226
	Tekle Haymanot	1215 - 1313
	Meister Eckhart	1260 - 1328
	Ignatius Loyola	1491 - 1556
	John of the Cross	1542 - 1591
	Francis de Sales	1567 - 1622
	Seraphim Sarov	1754 - 1833
	Patrick of Ireland	

CHAPTER 1
St Benedict of Nursia

"He should know that whoever undertakes the government of souls must prepare himself to account for them." – Saint Benedict of Nursia

CHAPTER 1 - St Benedict of Nurcia

Born:	480 AD
Died:	543 AD
Nationality:	Italian
Location:	Monte Casino
Outlook:	Catholic
Scribe:	Pope Gregory
Books:	The Rule of Saint Benedict
Interests:	Monastic government & Qualifications of leadership
Achievements:	Founder of Benedictine order
Key Teachings:	"Ora et Labora"– Prayer and Work
Supernatural Miracles:	Words of Prophecy, Words of Knowledge
Canonized:	1220

The Life of Benedict

"The sleepy like to make excuses", very little is known about the life of Saint Benedict, due to the early era of his life, and the time he served the church was especially sparse in the recording of his life.

Benedict was born in Norcia, Umbria, Odoacer's Kingdom in 480 AD to a Roman noble family.

At the age of 20, he left to study at Rome, however in seeing what Rome had to offer, he became a hermit in the town of Enfide about 40 miles from Rome.

Benedict met Romanus of Subiaco, a monk who had a monastery in the Simbruini Mountains, and he decided to stay in a cave below the monastery. He stayed in the cave for 3 years, being served by the monk who brought him food and company on a regular basis. Upon the death of Romanus, the other monks he led at the monastery asked Benedict to lead them; he however refused the offer, understanding that their lifestyle would not suit his hermetic style of living.

After that, the relationship between Benedict and the monks turned sour, and they tried to poison him with food and wine. In 530 Benedict thus left the monastery and founded 12 other communities in the area of Subiaco. In the late part of 530, Saint Benedict founded his monastery at Monte Cassio, between Rome and Naples.

His most famous accomplishment is the "Rule of Saint Benedict", which described the conduct of monks under his care. Many consider this work to be an adaptation of "The Rule of the Master", by John Cassian, who it is believed, received most of his insight from his travels to the desert fathers of Egypt.

Saint Benedict seems to be a contemporary of Pope Gregory, hence most of the information is derived from the Pope's Book 4 – Dialogues written in 593. The information in the work is not exact, as most of the information was received from some of the Benedict's disciples, and the stories they could tell.

Exact dates and times seem to be scarce, however the main character authenticity remains.

It seems Benedict died at the age of 66 on 21 March 547, at Monte Cassio monastery.

The life and writings of Saint Benedict of Monte Cassino

"Idleness is the enemy of the soul; and therefore, the brethren ought to be employed in manual labor at certain times, at others, in devout reading."
Saint Benedict

The "Rule of Saint Benedict" was written in 516, for the monks living together in monastic communities. The Rule has 73 chapters and focuses on two subjects, how to live a "Christocentric" life, and how to administrate a monastery.

Herewith is some of the oral history as told to Pope Gregory I. Most believe that the accounts are true, after all, who lies to a Pope, right? I trust you enjoy the miracles and stories as much as I do, I believe even if half of them are embellishments he was still a remarkable man.

Quoted below, from the work of Pope Gregory I, are done in two ways; the first with some extracts of the Rule written by Saint Benedict and the second will be some extracts of the miraculous stories of his life.

The Rule of Saint Benedict can be divided into three sections. (Ora Et Labora)

- Explaining the "Opus Dei"; the liturgy of the hours of the day.

- The Life of Vows; explaining the major themes of the Rule. Stability, Obedience and Conversion of manners.

- Overview of the Rule (the monastic rule of the order).

Ora et Labora

The Rule of Saint Benedict – Page 38 – Introduction

We are therefore now about to institute a school of the service of God; in which we hope nothing will be ordained rigorous or burdensome. But if in some things we proceed with a little severity, sound reason so advising, for the amendment of vices or preserving of charity; do not straightway for fear thereof, flee from the way of salvation which is always strait and difficult in the beginning. But in the process of time and growth of faith, when the heart has once been enlarged, the way of God's

commandments are run with unspeakable sweetness of love; so that, never departing from His teaching, but persevering in the Monastery in His doctrine until death, we share now by patience in the sufferings of Christ, that we may deserve afterwards to be partakers of His kingdom.

The Rule of Saint Benedict – Page 46 – Obedience to leaders

This obedience will then be acceptable to God and pleasing to men, if what is commanded be not done fearfully, slowly, coldly, or with murmuring, or an answer showing unwillingness; because the obedience which is given to superiors is given to God, Who hath said: "He that heareth you, heareth Me." Hence, it ought to be done by the disciples with a good will, because God "loveth a cheerful giver." If the disciple obeys with ill-will and murmur, not only in words, but also in heart, although he fulfils what is commanded him, it will not be acceptable to God, Who considereth the heart of the murmurer. For such a work, he shall not have any reward, but rather incurreth the penalty of murmurers, unless he amends and makes satisfaction.

The Rule of Saint Benedict – Page 47 – Silence

LET us act in accordance with that saying of the Prophet; "I have said: I will keep my ways, that I offend not with my tongue. I have been watchful over my mouth: I held my peace and humbled myself, and was silent from speaking even good things." If therefore, according to this saying of the Prophet, we are at times to abstain, for silence sake, even from good talk, how much more ought we to refrain from evil words, on account of the penalty of sin. Therefore, because of the importance of silence, let leave to speak be seldom given, even to perfect disciples, although their words be of good and holy matters, tending unto edification; because it is written: "In much speaking, thou shalt not escape sin." And in another place: "Death and life are in the hands of the tongue." For it befitteth a master to speak and teach; and it beseemeth a disciple to hold his peace and listen. If, therefore, anything must be asked of the Prior, let it be done with all fitting humility and the subjection of reverence. But as for buffoonery, idle words or such as move to laughter, we utterly condemn and exclude them in all places, nor do we allow a disciple to open his mouth to five them utterance.

The Rule of Saint Benedict – Page 47 – Humility, 1st Degree

The first degree, then, of humility is that a man always have the fear of God before his eyes, and altogether fly forgetfulness. Moreover to be mindful of all that God hath commanded and remember that such as contemn God fall into hell for their sins, and that everlasting life is prepared for such as fear Him.

The Rule of Saint Benedict – Page 48 – Humility, 2nd to 4th Degree

The second degree of humility is, if anyone, not wedded to his own will, seeks not to satisfy his desires, but carries out that saying of our Lord: "I came not to do My own Will, but the Will of Him Who sent Me." The scripture likewise saith: "Self-will engendereth punishment and necessity purchaseth a crown."

The third degree of humility is, that a man submits himself for the love of God, with all obedience to his superior, imitating thereby our Lord, of Whom the Apostle saith: "He was made obedient even unto death."

The fourth degree of humility is, that if, in obedience, things that are hard, contrary, and even unjust be done to him, he embraces them with a quiet conscience, and in suffering them, grow not weary, nor give over, since the Scripture saith: "He only that persevereth to the end shall be saved." And again, "Let thy heart be comforted and expect the Lord."

The Rule of Saint Benedict – Page 49 – Humility, 5th Degree

The fifth degree of humility is to manifest to the Abbot, by humble confession, all the evil thoughts of his heart, and the secret faults committed by him. The Scripture exhorteth us thereunto, saying: "Reveal thy way to the Lord, and hope in Him." And again: "Confess thy way to the Lord because He is good, because His mercy endureth for ever."

The Rule of Saint Benedict – Page 49 – Humility, 6th to 10th Degree

The sixth degree of humility is, if a Monk be content with all that is meanest and poorest, and in everything enjoined him, think himself an evil and worthless servant, saying with the Prophet: "I have been brought to nothing and knew it not. I have become as a beast before Thee, and I am always with Thee."

The seventh degree of humility is, not only to pronounce with his tongue, but also in his very heart to believe himself to be the most abject, and inferior to all; and humbling himself, to say with the Prophet: "I am a worm and no man, the reproach of men and the outcast of the people. I have been exalted, humbled, and confounded." And again: "It is good for me that Thou hast humbled me, that I may learn thy commandments."

The eighth degree of humility is, that a Monk do nothing but what the common rule of the Monastery or the examples of his seniors, exhort him to do.

The ninth degree of humility is, for a Monk to refrain his tongue from speaking, and be silent till a question be asked him, remembering the saying of the Scripture: "In many words thou shalt not avoid sin" and "a talkative man shall not be directed upon the earth."

The tenth degree of humility is, not to be easily moved and prompt to laugh, for it is written: "The fool exalteth his voice to laughter."

The Rule of Saint Benedict – Page 48 – Humility, 11th and 12th Degree

The eleventh degree of humility is that when a Monk speaketh, he does so, gently and without laughter; humbly, with gravity or few words, and discreetly; and be not clamorous in his voice; for it is written: "A wise man is known by few words."

The twelfth degree of humility is, that a Monk not only have humility in his heart, but show it also in his exterior, to all who behold him; so that whether he be at the work of God, in the Oratory, the monastery, the garden, on the way, in the field or wherever he may be, whether he sits, walks, or stands, let him always, with head bent down, and eyes fixed upon the earth, think of himself guilty for his sins, and about to be presented before the dreadful judgment of God, ever saying to himself with the Publican in the Gospel: "Lord, I am a sinner, not worthy to lift up mine eyes to heaven." And again with the Prophet: "I am bowed down and humbled on every side."

The Rule of Saint Benedict – Page 53 – Work

In what manner the Work of God is to be done in the day time.

"SEVEN times a day", saith the Prophet. "have I sung praises unto Thee." 160 This sacred number of seven shall be accomplished by us if at the times of Lauds, Prime, Tierce, Sext, None, Even-song, and Complin, we perform the duties of our service. It was of these hours the Prophet said: "Seven times in the day I have sung praise to Thee." For of the Night-watches, the same Prophet says: "At midnight I did arise to confess to Thee." At these times therefore, let us give praise to our Creator for the judgments of His justice;

that is at Lauds, Prime, Tierce, Sext, None, Even-song, and Complin; and in the night let us rise to confess unto Him.

The Rule of Saint Benedict – Page 55 – Prayer

Of reverence at prayer.

IF, when we wish to make some suggestion to the powerful, we presume not to speak to them except with humility and reverence; with how much greater reason ought we to present our supplications in all humility and purity of devotion, to the Lord God of all things? And let us bear in mind, that

we shall be heard, not for our many words, but for our purity of heart, and our penitential tears. Our prayer, therefore, ought to be short and pure, unless perchance it be prolonged by the inspiration of Diving Grace. Yet, let all prayer made in common be short, and when the sign has been given by the Prior, let all rise together.

The Rule of Saint Benedict – Page 67 – Labor

Of daily manual labor.

IDLENESS is an enemy of the soul. Therefore, the Brethren ought to be employed at certain times in laboring with their hands, and at other fixed times in holy reading. Wherefore we think that both these occasions may be well-ordered thus: From Easter till the first of October, let them, on going forth from Prime, labor at whatever they are required till about the fourth hour. From the fourth, till close upon the sixth hour, let them be employed in reading. On rising from table after the sixth hour, let them rest on their beds with all silence, or if perchance any one shall desire to read, let him read in such a way as not to disturb any one else.

Let None be said seasonable, at about the middle of the eighty hour, and after that let them work at what they have to do till the evening. If the situation of the place, or their poverty require them to labor in reaping their corn, let them not be saddened thereat, for then are they Monks in very deed, when they live by the labor of their hands, as our Fathers and the Apostles did before us. Yet let all things be done with moderation for the sake of the fainthearted.

The Rule of Saint Benedict – Page 69 – Hospitality

Of the manner of entertaining guests.

LET all guests who come to the Monastery be entertained like Christ Himself, because He will say: "I was a stranger and ye took Me in." 187 Let due honor be paid to all, especially to those who are of the household of the Faith, and to travellers. As soon, therefore, as a guest is announced, let the Prior or the Brethren go to meet him with all show of charity. First let them pray together, and so be associated to each other in peace. The kiss of peace shall not be offered till after prayer, because of the illusions of the devil. And in the salutation itself let all humility be shewn. By bowing the head or prostrating on the ground before all the guests who come or go, let Christ Who is received in their persons be also adored in them.

The Rule of Saint Benedict – Page 80 – Rule created for Beginners

That the whole observance of perfection is not contained in this Rule.

WE have written this Rule, that by its observance in Monasteries, we may show that we possess, in some measure, uprightness of manners, or the beginning of a good Religious life. But for such as hasten forward to the perfection of holy living, there are the precepts of the holy Fathers, the observance whereof leadeth a man to the height of perfection. For what page, or what passage is there in the divinely inspired books of the Old and New Testament, that is not a most perfect rule of man's life? Or what book is there of the holy Catholic Fathers that doth not proclaim this; that we may by a direct course reach our Creator? Moreover, what else are the Collations of the Fathers, their Institutes, their Lives, also the Rule of our Holy Father Basil, but examples of the good living and obedience of Monks, and so many instruments of virtue? But to us who are slothful and lead bad and negligent lives, they are matter for shame and confusion. Therefore, whosoever thou art that dost hasten to the heavenly country, first accomplish, by the help of Christ, this little Rule written for beginners.

The Miracles of Saint Benedict

Life of Saint Benedict – Page 6

And therefore, when they perceived themselves restrained from unlawful acts, it grieved them to leave their desires, and hard it was to relinquish old customs and begin a new life, besides the conversation of good men is always odious to the wicked, they began therefore to plot his death, and after consultation had together, they poisoned his wine. So when the glass which contained the empoisoned drink was, according to the custom of the Monastery, presented at the table to be blessed by the Abbot, Benedict putting forth his hand and making the sign of the Cross, the glass which was held far off brake in pieces, as if instead of blessing the vase of death, he had thrown a stone against it. By this the man of God perceived that the glass had in it the drink of death which could not endure the sign of life. So presently rising up with a mild countenance and tranquil mind, having called the Brethren together, he thus spoke unto them: "Almighty God of His mercy forgive you, Brethren, why have you dealt thus with me? Did not I foretell you that my manner of life and yours would not agree? Go, and seek a Superior to your liking; for you can no longer have me with you." This said, he forthwith returned to the solitude he loved as well and lived there with himself, in the sight of Him who seeth all things.

Life of Saint Benedict – Page 9

How by the prayer of the man of God a spring issued from the top of a mountain.

THREE of the Monasteries, which he founded in that place, were built upon the cliffs of a mountain, which was very troublesome to the Monks always to be forced to descend to the lake to fetch up their water, for on account of the steepness of the mountain side, it was very difficult and dangerous to descend. Hereupon the Brethren of these three Monasteries came together to the servant of God Benedict saying: "It is very troublesome to us to have daily to go down for water as far as the lake, and therefore the Monasteries must of necessity be removed to some more commodious place." He dismissed them with comfortable words, and at night with little Placidus, whom we mentioned before, went up to the rock and there prayed a long time. Having ended his prayers, he put three stones for a mark in the same place, and so unknown to all he returned to his Monastery. Next day, when the Brethren came again to him for want of water he said: "Go, and on the rock where you shall find three stones one upon another, dig a little, for Almighty God is able to make water spring from the top of that mountain, that you may be eased of this labor." When they had made a hollow in that place, it was immediately filled with water, which issueth forth so plentifully that to this day it continueth running down to the floor of the mountain.

Life of Saint Benedict – Page 9

How the iron head of a bill from the bottom of the water returned to the handle again.

AT another time, a certain Goth poor of spirit, desirous to lead a religious life, repaired to the man of god, Benedict, who most willingly received him. One day he ordered a bill to be given to him to cut up brambles in a place which he intended for a garden. This place, which the Goth had undertaken to accommodate, was over the lake's side. While the Goth labored amain in the cutting up the thick briars, the iron, slipping out of the handle, fell into the lake in a place so deep, that there was no hope to recover it. The Goth, having lost his bill, ran trembling to the Monk Maurus, and told him the mischance, confessing his fault penitently, who presently advertised Benedict the servant of God thereof. Immediately the man of God came himself to the lake, took the haft out of the Goth's hand, and case it into the lake, when, behold, the iron rose up from the bottom and entered into the haft as before. Which he there rendered to the Goth saying: "Behold! work on and be not discomforted."

Life of Saint Benedict – Page 9

How his disciple Maurus walked on the water.

The Life of Our most Holy Father S. Benedict Gregory the Great

ONE day as venerable Benedict was in his cell, the aforesaid young Placidus, a Monk of the holy man, went out to the lake to fetch water, and letting down the bucket to take up water, by chance fell in himself after it, and was presently carried away by the stream, a bow's shoot from the side. This accident was at the same time revealed to the man of God in his cell, who quickly called Maurus, saying: "Run, brother Maurus, for the child who went to fetch water is fallen into the lake, and the stream hath carried him a great way." A wonderful thing and not heard of since the time of Peter the Apostle! Maurus having asked and received his benediction, upon the command of his Superior went forth in haste, and, being come to the place to which the child was driven by the stream, thinking still he went upon the dry land he ran upon the water, shook him by the hair of the head, and returned speedily back. No sooner had he foot upon firm ground but he came to himself, and perceiving that he had gone upon the water, much astonished, he wondered how he had done that which wittingly he durst not adventure. So, returning to his Superior, he related what had happened, which the venerable man Benedict ascribed to Maurus his prompt obedience, and not to his own merits; but contrariwise Maurus attributed it wholly to his command, not imputing any virtue to himself in that which he had done unwittingly. This humble and charitable contention, the child who was saved, was to decide, for he said: "When I was drawn out of the water, methought I saw my Abbot's garments over my head and imagined that he had drawn me out.

Life of Saint Benedict – Page 12

How the man of God by his prayer, removed a huge stone.

ONE day, as the brethren were building the cells of the Cloister, there lay a stone in the midst which they determined to lift up and put into the building. When two or three were not able to move it, they set more to it, but it remained just as immoveable as if it had been held by roots to the ground, so that it was easy to conceive that the old enemy sat upon it, since that so many men were not able to lift it. After much labour in vain, they sent to the man of God to help them with his prayers to drive away the enemy, who presently came, and having first prayed, he gave his blessing, when behold the stone was as easily lifted as if it had not weight at all.

Life of Saint Benedict – Page 13

How a boy crushed by the fall of a wall was healed by the servant of God.

Scarce had the messenger told his errand when the malignant spirit overthrew the wall that was a building, and with the fall thereof crushed a young monk, son to a certain Senator. Hereat all of them much grieved and discomforted, not for the loss of the wall but for the harm to their brother, brought the heavy tidings to their venerable Father Benedict, who bid them bring the boy to him, who could not be carried but in a sheet, by reason that not only his body was bruised but also his bones crushed with the fall. Then the man of God willed them to lay him in his cell upon his mat where he used to pray; so causing the Brethren to go out he shut the door, and with more than ordinary devotion fell to his prayers. A wonder to hear, the very same hour he sent him to his work again, whole and sound as ever he was before, to help his Brethren in making up the wall; whereas the old enemy hoped to have had occasion to insult over Benedict for his death.

Life of Saint Benedict – Page 15

How he prophesied to King Totila and to the Bishop of Canosa.

THEN Totila came himself to the man of God, whom as soon as he saw sitting afar off, he durst not come nigh, but fell prostrate to the ground. The holy man twice of three bade him rise, but he durst not get up, then Benedict, the servant of Jesus Christ our Lord, deigned himself to come to the prostrate king, whom, raising from the ground, he rebuked for his deeds, and foretold in a few words all that should befall him saying: "Much evil dost thou do, and much wickedness hast thou done, as least now give over thy iniquity. Into Rome shalt thou enter, thou wilt cross over the sea, nine years shalt thou reign, and die the tenth." At the hearing whereof the king sore appalled, craved his prayers and departed, but from that time he was less cruel. Not long after he went to Rome, sailed thence to Sicily, and in the tenth year of his reign, by the judgment of Almighty God, lost both crown and life,

Life of Saint Benedict – Page 18

How St. Benedict discovered the hiding of a flagon of wine.

OUR monk Exhilaratus, whom you know well, on a time was sent by his master with two wooden vessels (which we call flagons) full of wine, to the man of god in his Monastery. He brought one but hid the other in the way, notwithstanding, the man of God, although he was not ignorant of anything done in his absence, received it thankfully, and advised the boy as he was returning back, in this manner: "Take care, son, thou drink not of that flagon which thou hast hid, but turn the mouth of it downward and then thou wilt perceive what is in it." He departed from the holy man much ashamed, and desirous to make further trial of what he had heard, held the flagon downwards, and presently there came forth a snake, at which the boy was sore affrighted and terrified for the evil he had committed.

Life of Saint Benedict – Page 19

How the man of God understood the proud thought of one of his Monks.

ONE day as the venerable Father late in the evening was at his repast, it happened that one of his Monks, the son of a lawyer, held the candle to him; and whilst the man of God was eating, he standing in that manner, began by the suggestion of pride to say within himself, "Who is he whom I should wait upon at the table or hold the candle unto with such attendance? Who am I who should serve him?" To whom the man of God presently turning, checked him sharply saying: "Sign thy breast, Brother, what is this you say? Sign thy breast." Then he forthwith called upon the Brethren and willed them to take the candle out of his hand, and bade him for that time to leave his attendance and sit down quietly by him. The Monk being asked afterward of the Brethren concerning his thoughts at that time, fold them how he was puffed up with a spirit of pride and what he spoke against the man of god secretly in his own heart. By this it was easily to be perceived that nothing could be kept from the knowledge of venerable Benedict, in whose ears the words of unspoken thoughts resounded.

Life of Saint Benedict – Page 20

How by a vision, he gave the order to construct The Monastery of Terracina.

At another time, he was requested by a certain devout man to send some of his disciples to build a Monastery on his estate near the city of Terracina. To which request he consented and sent some Monks, appointing an Abbot and Prior over them. As they were setting forward, he promised, saying: "Go, and upon such a day I will come and show you where to build the Oratory, where the Refectory and lodging for the guests, or what else shall be necessary." So they received his blessing and departed, in hope to see him at the appointed day, for which they prepared all tings they thought fit and necessary for their

Gather and his company. The night before the appointed day the man of God appeared in sleep to him whom, he had constituted Abbot and to his Prior, and described to them most exactly how he would have the building ordered. When they awaked, they related to each other what they had seen, yet not altogether relying upon that vision, they expected the man of God according to his promise, but seeing he came not at his appointed time, they returned to him very pensive, saying: "We have expected, Father, your coming, as you promised, but you came not to show us where and what we should build." To whom he said: "Why, Brethren, why do you say so? Did not I come according to my promise?" And when they said: "When came you?" he replied: "Did I not appear to each of you in your sleep and describe every place? Go, and according to the direction given you in that vision construct the Monastery." Hearing this they were much astonished, and so, returning to the manor, they erected the whole building according to the revelation.

Life of Saint Benedict – Page 27

To whom the man replied: "He is dead, come and raise him." When the servant of God heard this he was much grieved, and said: "Go, Brethren, go! This is not a work for us, but such as were the holy Apostles. Why will you impose burdens upon us which we cannot bear?" Notwithstanding, the man enforced with excessive grief, persisted in his petition, swearing that he would not depart unless he raised his son to life. Then the servant of God enquired, saying: "Where is he?" He answered: "Lo! h

His body lieth at the Monastery Gate." Whither when the man of God with his Brethren was come, he knelt down and laid himself on the body of the child; then, raising himself and with his hands held up towards Heaven, he prayed: "O Lord, regard not my sins, but the faith of this man who craveth to have his son restored to life, and restore again to this body the soul which thou hast taken from it." Scarce had he finished these words, but all the body of the boy began to tremble at the re-entry of the soul, so that in the sight of all who were present he was seen with wonderful quaking to pant and breathe. Whom he presently took by the hand and delivered alive and sound to his father.

It seemth to me, Peter, he had not this miracle actually in his power, which he prostrated himself to obtain by prayer.

Learning with Benedict

God loves all His children, and He loves and wants His children to love each other. "Benedict is a beloved in heaven. He remains praying for those who would seek Me with a pure heart, his time in heaven could be spent on other matters, yet he spends his time here looking for those on earth whom he can partner with, those who would seek Me at any cost." What an incredible introduction by Jesus! Benedict loves the mystic.

I was taught about circadian rhythms; I did not even know what the word meant, by this astounding man. He explained that the reason for most of the Rule, was to mimic this rhythm, which is found everywhere in nature. This very act of allowing the day to follow this pattern, allows one to elevate the understanding and awareness slowly, without the push-and-jerk patterns of many other meditations.

He explained how God had revealed this pattern in nature to him, and how by understanding this pattern, one can develop this more in our era to build on the contemplative practice of prayer.

Benedict has a great intimacy focus and his reason is that the men who will change the future on earth will be birthed in the fires of intimacy. Few can sustain this place of intimacy, and remain in the quiet place, focused on Jesus. Those who would remain, as long as possible in this place would have the greatest impact on their society, not based on human measurements, but the mere reality of a human soul, completely focused, surrendered to the eternal love gaze of Jesus.

Benedict loves a heart fully surrendered to God, who would be tender to the divine will, the divine inclinations, as one who would move on the mere breeze of the spirit, not requiring a tempest, or storms of life to adjust their course of action.

Benedict took me to a seashore, it was filled with gemstones, the whole beach just had stones of many colors, each shining with brilliance. He looked at me and said, these gems are the moments God treasures with us, His children. This place represents every time a saint on earth chose to spend time with God, chose God over everything else. You think the treasures of God, are the same as your treasures on earth.

God treasures relationship with humanity more than most would ever understand, the price of the Cross, the price paid by Jesus, was to have this place filled with these moments again, where God's love, melted with the human heart creates beauty beyond words, beyond riches, where the divine dance between God and His children, start vibrating the frequency of awe, adoration, love and encounter.

This place was expensive to recover; it cost Jesus His life, and I will co-labor with Jesus to recover the human heart, to populate heaven not just with souls, but to populate this shore of treasure with this divine interaction.

I stood on the shore, tears filled my eyes, I never knew how much God treasured every moment, every second, my heart was turned toward him, and there was an interaction between us, even a quick prayer in between my meetings at work, the times when I sneaked off to get coffee and thank God for answering my prayers, or just helping me with a problem I was wrestling with in the office.

There was no end to this seashore; my eyes could not see the end, the horizon was filled with gemstones.

Benedict looked at me, he smiled once again, the Father of heaven loves us more than most of us are even able to believe. We have become orphans trapped in the prison of pain. The prison created by a world taught us all the wrong ways to deal with pain and hurt, to "protect" your heart, yet in this place, there is no more separation. Abba Father wants to express Himself; He believes His love can heal the hurt of the world, and His Sons and Daughters can love again, with reckless abandon, and experience Him.

Benedict's brown monk's robe started to glitter. I saw how the very robe he was wearing was completely filled with these gemstones. His heart started to shine through the cloak, and said that the relationship with God, changes the character of the heart, when the heart shines from the inside and these patterns of character shine on the gemstones of your robe, your true priesthood is displayed.

The beauty and glory of God would shine into all the realms, as our heart mingled with the treasure of His heart, to display the goodness of God to the creation, bringing glory to God.

"Where your treasure is, there your heart will also be."

QUESTIONS

1. What part of his life, resonates with you?

2. Which of the extract of Benedict of Nursia writing did you enjoy the most?

3. Which of his miracles inspire you the most, do you think God still does miracles?

4. Do you think you could spend more time in your schedule with God?

5. If you could spend 10 minutes with God each day, what would you do with Him?

CHAPTER 2
Saint Francis of Assisi

*"If you have men who will exclude
any of God's creatures from
the shelter of compassion and pity,
you will have men who will
deal likewise with their
fellow men." – Francis of Assisi*

CHAPTER 2 – Saint Francis of Assisi

Born:	1181
Died:	1226
Nationality:	Italian
Location:	Assisi
Outlook:	Catholic
Books:	Canticle of the Sun
	Prayer before the Crucifix
	Regula non bullata, the Earlier Rule, 1221
	Regula bullata, the Later Rule, 1223
	Testament, 1226
	Admonitions
Interests:	Mystic
Achievements:	Founder of the Franciscan Order
Key Teachings:	The Motherhood of God – Jesus, The Passion of Christ
Supernatural Miracles:	Stigmata (Wounds of the Cross), Healings, Signs, and Wonders
Canonized:	16 July 1228

The Life of Saint Francis of Assisi

"Pure, holy simplicity confounds all the wisdom of this world and the wisdom of the flesh." - Francis of Assisi

Saint Francis of Assisi was born in 1182, in Assisi Italy to Pietro di Bernardone dei Moriconi, a French silk trader and his French mother, Pica de Bourlemont, from a noble family in Provence in France.

Francis lived the life of a spoilt brat. He lived like a hedonist, using the money from his family to fund his social life. He had several disagreements with his father, due to his nonchalant approach to the family business.

In 1202 he took part in a military campaign against Perugia. This resulted in him spending a year as a prisoner of war in Collestrada, where it is believed he had a slow spiritual conversion, returning after a year in prison.

In 1205, after another failed military excursion, he returned to Assisi, and then left for Rome, where he started begging at St. Peter's Basilica. Francis had his epiphany at San Damiano chapel, while praying he felt the Icon Jesus asking him to restore the chapel.

He also had another argument with his father, which resulted in him forgoing his inheritance, during legal proceedings, led by the Bishop of Assisi.

Francis spent the next 2 years begging for stones from the towns people, he restored many chapels in rural areas around Assisi. He also started taking care of the poor and nursing lepers in colonies around Assisi.

In 1208, upon hearing a sermon of the great commission, from Mass in the chapel of St. Mary of the Angels, he decided to dedicate his life to the poor and made a vow of poverty for the rest of his life.

Taking the clothes of the local peasants, he put on a brown tunic, and tied a rope around his waist, and started preaching and teaching in the rural villages around Assisi without any ordination or direction from spiritual authorities.

In 1209, with 11 followers, living at a leper colony at Rivo Torto near Assisi, he wrote the rule of his order. The Rule of Saint Francis is known as the "Regula Primitive" or "Primitive Rule". Which basically means; "To follow the teachings of our Lord Jesus Christ and to walk in His footsteps."

Francis wanted to create a new order, to do this, he needed to ask permission and blessing from the Pope, an audience with the Pope in Rome was not an easy matter to arrange.

When Francis came to Rome with his disciples, they met with Giovanni di San Paolo, the Cardinal Bishop of Sabina, who was also the confessor of Pope Innocent III, he immediately recognized the need for Francis to meet the Pope, and understood the value of their order as the will of God, while hearing about their revelation, the Cardinal was convinced of the divine sanction, and committed to arranging the meeting.

Giovanni di San Paolo, the Cardinal Bishop, arranged a meeting with the Pope. The Pope agreed to legitimize the Franciscan Order and officially get Papal authentication, on an informal basis, due to their number. But once the Franciscan order was substantial enough, the order would be made more formal.

Francis chose never to be ordained as a priest; however, he was later ordained as a deacon of the catholic church. Another order "The Lessor Brothers", was also started by Francis at the same time; they preached to the laity in Porziuncola and preached first in Umbria, later expanding their reach to the rest of Italy.

Francis preached at the church of San Rufino in Assisi in 1211, the noblewoman Clare of Assisi, becoming enraptured by his teaching, decided to follow her destiny, giving up her nobility and riches to heed the call of God.

On 28 March 1212, at Porziuncola, Italy, Francis received Clare and founded the Order of Poor Ladies. She joined a Benedictine monastery until the order could provide a place for her to stay with her younger sister. Francis later moved Clare to San Damiano where they stayed in straw huts and were called the "Poor Clare's."

Saint Francis was passionate about following the "great commission", so he attempted an evangelistic pilgrimage to Jerusalem; however, after being shipwrecked he returned home to Assisi.

On 8 May 1213, Count Orlando di Chiusi, gave Francis the mountain of La Verna (Alverna) as a place to use to build a monastery and retreat center for his followers. Francis would later use this place as a prayer retreat area, where he would seek the face of God, away from the busy cities.

After a few failed travels, Francis set out in 1219 with a monk to Egypt to convert the Sultan of Egypt. The Sultan, al-Kamil, a nephew of Saladin, was encamped at Damietta in a military campaign against the Crusaders.

On 29 August 1219 Saint Francis approached the Sultan during a ceasefire agreement, very little information has been provided by both the Crusaders or the Muslim court about their meeting, the Sultan did not convert, however, it is reported that Francis was allowed to travel in the holy land, without fearing for the safety of his order, or the brothers serving God with him.

The governance of the order was given over by Francis in 29 September 1220, to Brother Peter Catani who died 5 months later, this burden was then handed over to Brother Elias as Vicar of Francis.

While praying on 14 September 1224, at the mountain of Verna, Francis received the stigmata, the Saint saw a Seraphim (6-winged angel,) on the cross, and received the 5 wounds of the cross.

Francis died at Porziuncola, on the 3 October 1226, while singing Psalm 142.

Psalm 142 NKJV

A maskil of David. When he was in the cave. A prayer.

I cry aloud to the LORD;

I lift up my voice to the LORD for mercy.

I pour out my complaint before him;

before him I tell my trouble.

When my spirit grows faint within me,

it is you who know my way.

In the path where I walk men have hidden a snare for me.

Look to my right and see;

no one is concerned for me.

I have no refuge;

no one cares for my life.

I cry to you, O LORD;

I say, "You are my refuge, my portion in the land of the living."

Listen to my cry,

for I am in desperate need;

rescue me from those who pursue me,

for they are too strong for me.

Set me free from my prison,

that I may praise your name.

Then the righteous will gather about me

because of your goodness to me.

Theology of Saint Francis of Assisi

"Holy charity confounds all diabolical and fleshly temptations and all fleshly fears." - Francis of Assisi

Although many consider Saint Francis a man of nature, it is clear his life speaks of many miracles, some of which are based on his relationship to nature, and the restoration of man's relationship to nature.

The miracle stories told below in a book about his life, written by Brother Ugolino, have been drawn into question, although I understand this criticism, I have tried to include only the stories I believe to be true, and which in my estimation, point towards a very specific lesion. Signs are after all there to point towards something, or to give us some direction to follow. The nature of his life was one of preaching the Gospel, we all know that the bible proclaims signs and wonders will follow those who preach the word of God.

Signs are made to make you wonder; they are supposed to confound the natural mind. I don't want to speak too much about the theological reasons behind the signs, or what they mean, I trust the Lord will reveal what is needed. Let us not stumble as we read these words, where our understanding is lacking, lets us exclaim, "the Lord is marvelous in all His ways, who can comprehend all His works", and then move on from there.

In a better sense than the antithesis commonly conveys, it is true to say that what St. Benedict had stored St. Francis scattered; but in the world of spiritual things what had been stored into the barns like grain was scattered over the world as seed. The servants of God who had been a besieged garrison became a marching army; the ways of the

world were filled as with thunder with the trampling of their feet and far ahead of that ever swelling host went a man singing; as simply he had sung that morning in the winter woods, where he walked alone."

G.K. Chesterton

Little Flowers – Page 25

Above all the graces and all the gifts of the Holy Spirit which Christ grants to his friends, is the grace of overcoming oneself, and accepting willingly, out of love for Christ, all suffering, injury, discomfort and contempt; for in all other gifts of God we cannot glory, seeing they proceed not from ourselves but from God, according to the words of the Apostle, 'What hast thou that thou hast not received from God? and if thou hast received it, why dost thou glory as if thou hadst not received it?' But in the cross of tribulation and affliction we may glory, because, as the Apostle says again, 'I will not glory save in the cross of our Lord Jesus Christ.' Amen."

Little Flowers – Page 33

Apostles Peter and Paul appeared to St Francis in much splendour, and thus addressed him: "As thy prayer and thy wish is to observe that which Christ and his holy Apostles observed, the Lord Jesus sends us to thee, to tell thee that thy prayer has been heard, and that it is granted to thee and to all thy followers to possess the treasure of holy poverty. We tell thee also from him, that whosoever, after thy example, shall embrace this holy virtue, shall most certainly enjoy perfect happiness in heaven; for thou and all thy followers shall be blessed by God." Having said these words they disappeared, leaving St Francis full of consolation. Then rising from prayer, and returning to Brother Masseo

Little Flowers – Page 34

In the beginning of the Order, St Francis, having assembled his companions to speak to them of Christ, in a moment of great fervour of spirit commanded one of them, in the name of God, to open his mouth and speak as the Holy Spirit should inspire him. The brother, doing as he was ordered, spoke most wonderfully of God. Then St Francis bade him to be silent and ordered another brother to speak in the same way, which having done with much penetration, St Francis ordered him likewise to be silent and commanded a third brother to do the same. This one began to speak so deeply of the things of God, that St Francis was convinced that both he and his companion had spoken through the Holy Spirit. Of which he also received a manifest proof;

for whilst they were thus speaking together, our Blessed Lord appeared in the midst of them, under the form of a beautiful young man, and blessed them all. And they, being ravished out of themselves, fell to the ground as if they had been dead, and were all unconscious of things external. And when they recovered from their trance, St Francis said to them: "My beloved brothers, let us thank God, who has deigned to reveal to the world, through his humble servants, the treasures of divine wisdom. For the Lord it is who openeth the mouth of the dumb, and maketh the tongues of the simple to speak wisdom."

Little Flowers – Page 35

The hour of dinner being arrived, St Francis and St Clare, with one of the brethren of St Francis and the sister who had accompanied the saint, sat down together, all the other companions of St Francis seated humbly round them. When the first dish was served, St Francis began to speak of God so sweetly, so sublimely, and in a manner so wonderful, that the grace of God visited them abundantly, and all were rapt in Christ. Whilst they were thus rapt, with eyes and hearts raised to heaven, the people of Assisi and of Bettona, and all the country round about, saw St Mary of the Angels as it were on fire, with the convent and the woods adjoining. It seemed to them as if the church, the convent, and the woods were all enveloped in flames; and the inhabitants of Assisi hastened with great speed to put out the fire. On arriving at the convent, they found no fire; and entering within the gates they saw St Francis, St Clare, with all their companions, sitting round their humble meal, absorbed in contemplation; then knew they of a certainty, that what they had seen was a celestial fire, not a material one, which God miraculously had sent to bear witness to the divine flame of love which consumed the souls of those holy brethren and nuns;

Little Flowers – Page 38

Wait for me here by the way, whilst I go and preach to my little sisters the birds"; and entering into the field, he began to preach to the birds which were on the ground, and suddenly all those also on the trees came round him, and all listened while St Francis preached to them, and did not fly away until he had given them his blessing. And Brother Masseo related afterwards to Brother James of Massa how St Francis went among them and even touched them with his garments and how none of them moved. Now the substance of the sermon was this: "My little sisters the birds, ye owe much to God, your Creator, and ye ought to sing his praise at all times and in all places, because he has given you liberty to fly about into all places; and though ye neither spin nor sew, he has given you a twofold and a threefold clothing for yourselves and for your offspring.

Little Flowers – Page 40

Approaching near to hear and see whence they came, he saw a great and wonderful light all round the saint, and in the light was Jesus Christ, with the Virgin Mary, St John the Baptist, St John the Evangelist and a great multitude of angels, all talking with St Francis. On seeing this, the child fell to the ground as if he had been dead. The miracle of this holy vision being ended, St Francis rose to return to the convent, and stumbling in the way against the child, who appeared to be dead, with great compassion he took him up in his arms and carried him in his bosom, as the good shepherd is wont to carry his lambs. Having learned from him how he had seen the vision, he forbade him to tell any man thereof so long as he, St Francis, lived

Little Flowers – Page 118

And being thus inflamed in that contemplation, on that same morning he beheld a seraph descending from heaven with six fiery and resplendent wings; and this seraph with rapid flight drew nigh unto St Francis, so that he could plainly discern him and perceive that he bore the image of one crucified and the wings were so disposed, that two were spread over the head, two were outstretched in flight, and the other two covered the whole body. And when St Francis beheld it, he was much afraid, and filled at once with joy and grief and wonder. He felt great joy at the gracious presence of Christ, who appeared to him thus familiarly, and looked upon him thus lovingly, but, on the other hand, beholding him thus crucified, he felt exceeding grief and compassion. He marveled much at so stupendous and unwonted a vision, knowing well that the infirmity of the Passion accorded ill with the immortality of the seraphic spirit. And in that perplexity of mind it was revealed to him by him who thus appeared, that by divine providence this vision had been thus shown to him that he might understand that, not by martyrdom of the body, but by a consuming fire of the soul, he was to be transformed into the express image of Christ crucified in that wonderful apparition.

Little Flowers – Page 119

St Francis an excessive fire and ardour of divine love, and on his flesh a wonderful trace and image of the Passion of Christ. For upon his hands and feet began immediately to appear the figures of the nails, as he had seen them on the Body of Christ crucified, who had appeared to him in the likeness of a seraph. And thus the hands and feet appeared pierced through the midst by the nails, the heads were seen outside the flesh in the palms of the hands and the soles of the feet, and the points of the nails stood out at the back of the hands, and the feet in such wise that they appeared to be twisted and bent back upon themselves, and the portion thereof that was bent back upon themselves, and the portion thereof that was bent back or twisted stood out free from the flesh, so that one could put a finger through the same as through a ring and the heads of the nails were round and black. In like manner, on the right side appeared the image of an unhealed wound, as if made by a lance, and still red and bleeding, from which drops of blood often flowed from the holy breast of St Francis, staining his tunic and his drawers.

Little Flowers – Page 121

As to the fourth consideration, be it known, that after the true love of Christ had perfectly transformed St Francis into God, and into the true image of Christ crucified, that angelical man, having fulfilled the Lent of forty days in honour of St Michael the Archangel on the holy mountain of Alvernia, came down from the mount with Brother Leo and a devout peasant, on whose ass he rode, because, by reason of the nails in his feet, he could hardly go on foot. And the fame of his sanctity being already spread abroad through the country by the shepherds who had seen Mount Alvernia on fire, and who took it to be a token of some great miracle wrought by God on his person.

Personal Journey with Saint Francis of Assisi

I have always loved my idea of Saint Francis, but Francis is not the normal mystic everybody wants him to be; the way he interacted with nature and the way he lived made him controversial, and his life has been woven into many agendas, I realized as I looked at his life.

My first question encountering him was thus, if he lived today, what would he say to this generation, how would he deal with the challenges we deal with today.

I expected a long explanation of hidden revelations, or something very different, but his words to me were so simple, "Look at my life son, look at how I lived, it will help you more than you know."

He continued to show me how he approached nature, every moment for him, was a place of conscious engagement, when he saw an animal, he took time to think about what that animal would consider important, he would look at an earthworm, and then think what things would an earthworm consider important, this exercise helped him imagine life in the macro and the micro.

Francis practiced conscious awareness and the present moment, in every little movement in nature, he was completely aware, living in that very moment, not thinking about the future, he carried as much honor for the worm as the king.

His heart's affections were not swayed by position or power. He realized this was a gift from God to him, and he used all his powers of focus, concentration, and silence to hear the whispers of the Divine in the sounds of nature.

He used his imagination to think about the small things and find lessons in the life of that animal, to him nature was the very cathedral of God. He showed me how every sound coming from creation, was able to speak, display and worship God, part of his understanding and relationship with nature was to understand how each creature expressed this worship.

We often approach nature to somehow subdue creation when God's original creation was meant to be tended. We place ourselves in opposition to nature, as if we need to conquer it when God says all creation worships Him. Nature is not just about the resources; we also need to replenish nature.

When Jesus died, He was the promise to creation, that the Son of God, would bring restoration, the death of Jesus changed the nature of creation from adversarial to co-laboring grace. Francis explained, once we deal with our death, once we realize, the fear of death is a mirage of an enemy already overcome by the Cross, like Apostle Paul writes, "Death where is your sting", we then approach all creation without the stench of death, but the fragrance of Christ, creation then responds to us, based on the divine nature we carry, and are able to be governed once again, like Adam did in the garden, tending the garden towards greater worship of God.

This tending to the garden requires a new kind of leader. Francis was concerned about the requirements for positions and the clamor of the body of Christ towards titles, and positions of power.

He spoke about his own life, how he always walked away from positions of power and false edifices of structures to create systems, and build institutions instead of building character in people. The early church leaders devoted themselves to prayer and the word, the apostles of Christ, prioritized the presence of God, over the "serving of tables."

We need to do the same when leading people; organization is not evil, but makes sure the administrators are not the ones carrying all the power, and all the ability to make decisions. Our leadership is always value-based, and people don't just learn by what we say, but by how we lead.

If leaders are able to spend time on the ground, with their feet in the grass, walking with people, showing them the simple way, teaching them to love the poor, showing them the how, and the why, not just concepts on presentation screens, not just videos on marketing boards, but real interaction, real social justice that require spiritual leaders to have to open their hearts and actually walk with the poor, speak to the broken, and love them with their own hands.

Christ very life was a life spent among the broken, destitute, and hungry souls of society. His school of theology was a "school of the knees", both serving the poor, and serving God, in prayer and power.

QUESTIONS

1. What part of his life, and her challenges you?

2. Considering that Saint Francis was a revolutionary in his era, what about his life do you think was most confrontational to the people around him?

3. Do you think there is somebody poor around you, which might need one meal today?

4. If being a follower of Jesus means spending time with the poor, what about the poor make them so repugnant to modern man?

5. Is there any long-term solutions society could look at to help the poor change the course of their lives, beyond just welfare?

6. What does the world look like without poor people?

CHAPTER 3
Ignatius of Loyola

*"If our church is not marked by
caring for the poor, the oppressed,
the hungry, we are guilty of heresy."
– Ignatius of Loyola*

Born:	1491
Died:	1556
Nationality:	Spanish
Location:	Rome
Outlook:	Catholic Jesuit Priest
Personal Secretary:	Juan Alfonso de Polanco
Books:	Spiritual exercises
	Autobiography de San Ignacio de Loyola (autobiography)
Interests:	Theology, Spiritual Direction
Achievements:	Co-founder society of Jesus
Key Teachings:	Discernment, Spiritual practice
Beatified:	27 July 1609
Canonized:	12 March 1622

The Life of Ignatius of Loyola

"He who goes about to reform the world must begin with himself, or he loses his labor." - St. Ignatius of Loyola

Ignatius was born on 23 October 1491 in Azpeitia, at the castle of Loyola in today's Gipuzkoa, Basque Country, Spain. The blacksmith's wife adopted Ignatius as his mother died soon after his birth and thus María de Garín became his mother.

As a young boy he worked as a page in the castle and assisted his relative, Juan Velázquez de Cuéllar, treasurer of the kingdom of Castile. He joined the military at the age of 17 years old and was known as a clavier brash young man, with an affinity for dressing well, and spending time with too many ladies. Ignatius committed many violent crimes at that time but avoided the law due to his station in life.

Once, when encountering a Moor who denied the divinity of Christ, he challenged him to a duel and killed the man. He also dueled with other men, surviving the duels, and thus killing his opponents.

In 1509 Ignatius started his military career formally by going into battle under Antonio Manrique de Lara, 2nd Duke of Nájera, where he grew as a natural leader with a diplomatic flair. He was injured at the battle of Pamplona in 1521, and the injury affected his leg. He would limp for the rest of his life, despite the best efforts of the surgeons at the time.

Due to his long recovery period, he was only able to read the scriptures, and other spiritual works, as the hospital was administrated and staffed by the church. Ignatius did not have access to his normal reading materials during this time. While reading the works, De Vita Christi, of Ludolph of Saxony he experienced a conversion. This work would later influence his own writing and his spiritual path.

Ignatius started his path of devotion at the Santa Maria de Montserrat. He gave up his fancy clothes, his sword, and military gear. After a time, he walked down the mountain from the monastery to a town called Manresa where he begged for a few months, volunteered at the local hospital and spent 7 hours a day practicing meditation and developing his spiritual exercise in the cave close to the town.

In 1523, Ignatius started his pilgrimage to Jerusalem, and after staying there for the most of September, his goal was to settle in the Holy land, however the bothers of the Franciscan order sent him back home.

At the age of 33 Ignatius enrolled in the grammar school at Barcelona, after having prepared himself for studies he enrolled at the University of Alcalá where he focused on theology and Latin from 1524 to 1534. After completing these studies, he moved to Paris where he studied at the ascetic Collège de Montague. Ignatius then progressed to the Collège Sainte-Barbe where he finished his Master of Arts degree in 1535.

In 1539 Ignatius founded the Society of Jesus with his two friends, Peter Faber and Francis Xavier. This was officially recognized by the Pope, and Ignatius was installed as the Father General by the Jesuits.

Ignatius dispatched his friends to create educational intuitions across Europe, and by doing this converted the population as missionary educators. Juan de Vega started a Jesuit college in Messina which proved to be a huge success and used this as a prototype elsewhere.

During 1553 to 1555, Ignatius Loyola dictated his autobiography to his male sectary, Father Gonçalves da Câmara, who published his version in Spanish.

Ignatius died from Malaria on the 31 July 1556, in Rome, he is currently buried at the Church of the Gesù.

Theology and Exerts from his Works

"It is dangerous to make everybody go forward by the same road: and worse to measure others by oneself."

St. Ignatius of Loyola

The fundamental contribution of Ignatius of Loyola was a work that depicted spiritual exercises for the Christian to follow. The aim of the theology is to develop within the believer an understanding of sin, in the context of their lives, and to understand and meditate on the gravity of sin, and the huge work of the Cross to deliver us from the problem of sin.

To the modern mind, these exercises look excessive, even strange, our idea of sin, and the nature of sin have changed in modern society. The reality is however, the consequences of our sin have not changed, hence my inclusion of these exercises. They also help one to imagine and meditate on the work of the Cross.

The Spiritual exercises divides the week into four movements:

- **The Purgative Way**
  - Man is created to worship God, revere, and serve Him.
  - Our starting point is being loved and accepted by God, and then examine what draws us away from God.

- **The Illuminative Way**
  - We ponder the kingship of Jesus, and then the mysteries of the last supper.

- **Unitive Way**
  - Focus on the passion of the Christ and the Cross.

- **Unitive Way continued**
  - The Joy of Christ and His risen life

One might look at the work below, and claim, why is this man called a mystic? But the underlying process, the thought behind this method, can only appreciated once tasted.

Do not for one moment look at these exercises as simple imaginings for a Jesuit order, and leave them to the annals of history. Behind the simplicity lies great treasures, as Ignatius is subtly teaching you to meditate on the scripture, to use the mind in the effort and pursuit of divinity.

Let not the examples on the pages limit you, use these same examples on the rest of scripture, and paint with a very broad bush the words you read here, be gracious to a man outside of your time, and use the skeleton of his thoughts, ideas and method, and add your own life, your own time and your own ideas. Soon you will see the brilliance of the man behind these words and the goodness of God who revealed this to him in a cave in Spain.

Spiritual Exercises – Page 23, Meditation: First Exercise

Here it is to be noted that, in a visible contemplation or meditation - as, for instance, when one contemplates Christ our Lord, Who is visible - the composition will be to see with the sight of the imagination the corporeal place where the thing is found which I want to contemplate. I say the corporeal place, as for instance, a Temple or Mountain where Jesus Christ or Our Lady is found, according to what I want to contemplate. In an invisible contemplation or meditation - as here on the Sins - the composition will be to see with the sight of the imagination and consider that my soul is imprisoned in this corruptible body, and all the compound in this valley, as exiled among brute beasts: I say all the compound of soul and body.

Spiritual Exercises – Page 23

The second is to ask God our Lord for what I want and desire.

The petition has to be according to the subject matter; that is, if the contemplation is on the Resurrection, one is to ask for joy with Christ in joy; if it is on the Passion, he is to ask for pain, tears and torment with Christ in torment.

Spiritual Exercises – Page 25, Typical Progression

Second Point

> *The second, to weigh the sins, looking at the foulness and the malice which any mortal sin committed has in it, even supposing it was not forbidden.*

Third Point

> *The third, to look at who I am, lessening myself by examples: First, how much I am in comparison to all men; Second, what men are in comparison to all the Angels and Saints of Paradise; Third, what all Creation is in comparison to God: (-then I alone, what can I be?); Fourth, to see all my bodily corruption and foulness; Fifth, to look at myself as a sore and ulcer, from which have sprung so many sins and so many iniquities and so very vile poison.*

Fourth Point

> *The fourth, to consider what God is, against Whom I have sinned, according to His attributes; comparing them with their contraries in me - His Wisdom with my ignorance; His Omnipotence with my weakness; His Justice with my iniquity; His Goodness with my malice.*

Fifth Point

> *The fifth, an exclamation of wonder with deep feeling, going through all creatures, how they have left me in life and preserved me in it;*

the Angels, how, though they are the sword of the Divine Justice, they have endured me, and guarded me, and prayed for me; the Saints, how they have been engaged in interceding and praying for me; and the heavens, sun, moon, stars, and elements, fruits, birds, fishes and animals - and the earth, how it has not opened to swallow me up, creating new Hells for me to suffer in them forever!

Spiritual Exercises – Page 31

Third Point. The third, those who will want to be more devoted and signalise themselves in all service of their King Eternal and universal Lord, not only will offer their persons to the labor, but even, acting against their own sensuality and against their carnal and worldly love, will make offerings of greater value and greater importance, saying:

"Eternal Lord of all things, I make my oblation with Thy favor and help, in presence of Thy infinite Goodness and in presence of Thy glorious Mother and of all the Saints of the heavenly Court; that I want and desire, and it is my deliberate determination, if only it be Thy greater service and praise, to imitate Thee in bearing all injuries and all abuse and all poverty of spirit, and actual poverty, too, if Thy most Holy Majesty wants to choose and receive me to such life and state."

Spiritual Exercises – Page 47, Complete Meditation on the Passover Meal

First Prelude.

> *The first Prelude is to bring to memory the narrative; which is here how Christ our Lord sent two Disciples from Bethany to Jerusalem to prepare the Supper, and then He Himself went there with the other Disciples; and how, after having eaten the Paschal Lamb, and having supped, He washed their feet and gave His most Holy Body and Precious Blood to His Disciples, and made them a discourse, after Judas went to sell his Lord.*

Second Prelude.

> *The second, a composition, seeing the place. It will be here to consider the road from Bethany to Jerusalem, whether broad, whether narrow, whether level, etc.; likewise the place of the Supper, whether large, whether small, whether of one kind or whether of another.*

Third Prelude.

> *The third, to ask for what I want. It will be here grief, feeling and confusion because for my sins the Lord is going to the Passion.*

First Point.

> *The first Point is to see the persons of the Supper, and, reflecting on myself, to see to drawing some profit from them.*

Second Point.

> *The second, to hear what they are talking about, and likewise to draw some profit from it.*

Third Point.

> *The third, to look at what they are doing and draw some profit.*

Fourth Point.

> *The fourth, to consider that which Christ our Lord is suffering in His Humanity, or wants to suffer, according to the passage which is being contemplated, and here to commence with much vehemence and to force myself to grieve, be sad and weep, and so to labor through the other points which follow.*

Fifth Point.

> *The fifth, to consider how the Divinity hides Itself, that is, how 1In His Humanity is in St. Ignatius' hand, correcting the Humanity of before Christ.*
>
> *It could destroy Its enemies and does not do it, and how It leaves the most sacred Humanity to suffer so very cruelly.*

Sixth Point.

> *The sixth, to consider how He suffers all this for my sins, etc.; and what I ought to do and suffer for Him.*

Spiritual Exercises – Page 54

The First Point is, to bring to memory the benefits received, of Creation,

Redemption and particular gifts, pondering with much feeling how much God our Lord has done for me, and how much He has given me of what He has, and then the same Lord desires to give me Himself as much as He can, according to His Divine ordination.

And with this to reflect on myself, considering with much reason and justice, what I ought on my side to offer and give to His Divine Majesty, that is to say, everything that is mine, and myself with it, as one who makes an offering with much feeling:

Take, Lord, and receive all my liberty, my memory, my intellect, and all my will -- all that I have and possess. Thou gavest it to me: to Thee, Lord, I return it! All is Thine, dispose of it according to all Thy will. Give me Thy love and grace, for this is enough for me.

Spiritual Exercises – Page 55, First Method of Prayer

The first Method of Prayer is on the Ten Commandments, and on the Seven Deadly Sins, on the Three Powers of the Soul and on the Five Bodily Senses. This method of prayer is meant more to give form, method and exercises, how the soul may prepare itself and benefit in them, and that the prayer may be acceptable, rather than to give any form or way of praying.

Spiritual Exercises – Page 56, Second Method of Prayer

It is by contemplating the meaning of each word of the Prayer. The Second Method of Prayer is that the person, kneeling or seated, according to the greater disposition in which he finds himself and as more devotion accompanies him, keeping the eyes closed or fixed on one place, without going wandering with them, says FATHER, and is on the consideration of this word as long as he finds meanings, comparisons, relish and consolation in considerations pertaining to such word. And let him do in the same way on each word of the OUR FATHER, or of any other prayer which he wants to say in this way.

Spiritual Exercises – Page 56, Third Method of Prayer

It will be by rhythm. The Third Method of Prayer is that with each breath in or out, one has to pray mentally, saying one word of the OUR FATHER, or of another prayer which is being recited: so that only one word be said between one breath and another, and while the time from one breath to another lasts, let attention be given chiefly to the meaning of such word, or to the person to whom he recites it, or to his own baseness, or to the difference from such great height to his own so great lowness. And in the same form and rule he will proceed on the other words of the OUR FATHER; and the other prayers, that is to say, the SOUL OF CHRIST, the CREED, and the HAIL, HOLY QUEEN, he will make as he is accustomed.

My Experience with Ignatius of Loyola

My first experience with Ignatius was during my first trip to Spain in 2018. It was a hot June day in the middle of summer in this beautiful country. We had just visited the monastery at Monserrat, and according to my research the town of Manresa was close to the train station, and I had read about Ignatius being in that town. We decided to go to Manresa!

After missing a train, trying to hitchhike to the town, then walking back to the station, then getting the right train, I was on my way to the place where Ignatius had most of his experiences with God, where he isolated himself in search of God.

After asking about 5 locals how to walk from the train station to the church, we finally found the cave, with the church built over it in later years. A typical old Spanish town, with a small church in comparison to the huge cathedral in the center of the town and the monastery we had just come from.

The cave is towards the side of the church, on the left as you enter the door. As I walked into the church, I could feel the realms and dimensions starting to dance around me, in the dimly lit cathedral; I walked towards the cave, and as I sat in the small room, on the wooden benches, the presence of God came rushing into the cave.

Ignatius introduced himself in the realms, a humble stately man, his stature in the realms was clear, he knew what he came to say. He spoke to me about his time in this place. And I realized while listening to him account some of the moments he had in the cave that this man came here to find God. I could really experience the moments of deep anguish, the prayer, the seeking, and his passion for Jesus. And I had the distinct feeling that he would not have left this place without having a personal life-changing experience with God.

We have all been at that place in our lives where we need to meet God face to face. Where anything less will not help us, where we are totally dependent on the presence of God to change us, our situations. A desperate clinging onto God for a breakthrough. This is a beautiful place of growth and one that I can see in this encounter, God cherishes. God says that if we seek him, He will let us find Him.

One of the first things I learned from Ignatius was the understanding that not everything that looks and feels simple is as simple as it seems. The need to exercise the imagination and learning to use your imagination to meditate on the word permeates his teaching, but also helped me see things in the scripture, I would have missed otherwise.

By learning how to use my mind to carefully work on the scripture, working on the words, seeing and experiencing the scripture with my imagination, helped me to experience the words. Soon I was growing into this, starting to experience the scriptures without my imagination; God took me into the scriptures in the spirit.

This was not done by my own effort; I would sit and pray, and suddenly find myself in the middle of the story, standing and watching the events unfold in history. It was like time opened to me, and I was able to experience moments in the scripture. Jesus would sit with me afterwards, and the Holy Spirit would explain certain truths and hidden meanings in the events, as I learned about the life of Jesus and other biblical characters.

The practices that I have learned from Ignatius have greatly helped my ability to engage with the Word and to focus my attention on the truths that have always been right before my eyes. Ignatius has an amazing ability to mentor the brethren that came to him for advice. The discipline that the exercises required helped him to be clear and directive in giving advice. He, while in this place of seeking God, received these exercises. There is so much treasure that God wants to give His children. The question remains, "Will we come to Him to receive."

QUESTIONS

1. Which part of his life do you find interesting?

2. From the extracts out of his spiritual exercises which one did you like?

3. Is there any of these spiritual exercises you could practice this week?

4. Could you spend some time alone in a cave with God?

5. Which ideas of Ignatius do you disagree with?

CHAPTER 4
Saint Ivan of Rila

"Just because of this I made up my mind to write for you this rough and ignorant testament of mine, so that you will keep it always in your minds to become stronger in body and soul, in the Lord, and go forward through the virtues in fear of God." – Ivan of Rila

Born:	876
Died:	946
Nationality:	Bulgaria
Location:	Rila Monastery
Outlook:	Eastern Orthodox church
Books:	Autobiography
Interests:	Writing, Theology
Key Teachings:	Prayer, Theology, ascetesism
Supernatural Miracles:	Healing

The Life of Saint Ivan Rilski of Rila

Ivan of Rila was born 876 AD, in Skrino at the Osogovo Mountain, Sardica Province, close to Dupnitsa city in modern Bulgaria.

Ivan was an orphan from a young age and lived a simple life because his parents died at an early age, leaving him behind with no-one to look after him. He was originally a cow herder, but at the age of 25, he became a priest at the St Dimitrii Monastery at the mountain peak of Ruen.

Ivan spent 12 years in the wilderness as an ascetic. He lived in a cave and spent those years praying and seeking God. After this period, he moved to the wilderness in the Rila Mountains, where he stayed in a hollow tree. Some of the local Shepperds started finding him on a regular basis, so he moved to a rocky outcrop on a cliff, to avoid becoming well-known.

He stayed on the cliff for 7 years. His disciples built a church in the cave where he formally dwelt, and after some time passed the church was converted into a formal monastery. He taught the monastics his, "divine way of life", and started mentoring them at this stage.

At one point during this time, King Peter the monarch of Bulgaria wanted to meet him, however; to avoid the fame, he declined the visit. Five years before his death he wrote his, "A Testament to the disciples."

On August 18, 946 Saint Ivan of Rila died at the age of 70. He is also known as St John of Rila.

Theology and Exerts from his Works

Testament of St John of Rila – Page 125

John, the humble and sinful, who has never done anything good on earth, when I came into this wilderness of Rila, I found no man over here, but only wild animals and impenetrable thick- ets. I settled alone in it among the wild animals, without food nor shelter, but the sky was my shelter and the earth my bed and the herbs my food. But the good Lord, for the love of whom I disregarded everything and endured hunger and thirst, frost, the heat of the sun, and corporal nakedness, did not abandon me, but like a merciful and child-loving father he lavishly satisfied all my needs. What shall I contribute to the Lord for all he has given me? Many are his benefactions to me, for he looked from his holy height at my humbleness (cf. Luke 1:48) and lent his support to me to go through everything—not I, but the might of Christ, which is in me—because every good gift and every perfect gift is from him (James 1:17).

Testament of St John of Rila – Page 131

Nor look to be recognized and beloved by earthly kings and princes, nor put your hope in them, leaving the heavenly King, with whom you enlisted to be soldiers and "wrestle not against flesh and blood," but "against the ruler of the darkness of this world" (Eph. 6:12). For the prophet Jeremiah also threatens us speaking so: "Cursed be the man that hopeth in man" and the rest. Enumerating the evils, he adds that "blessed is the man that hopeth in the Lord" (Jer. 17:5-8). Do not say: "What shall we eat, or drink, or in what shall we be dressed?" for the gentiles seek after these things. "Look at the birds of the air: for they neither sow nor reap, nor gather into barns; yet your heavenly father feeds them. Are you not of more value than they?" (Matt. 6:26). As soon as you have come out of the world, do not go back, neither with your body, nor with your mind, for, as it is said, "No man, having put his hand to the plough, and looking back, is fit for the Kingdom of Heaven" (Luke 9:62).

Testament of St John of Rila – Page 131

As the grace of the Holy Spirit brought you together, so must you endeavor to live with one heart and one mind and one spirit, directing your eyes only towards the eternal reward, which God has prepared for those who have loved him. The communal life is in every way more useful for monks than the solitary one, for solitude is not suitable for the many, but only for a few who are perfect in all monastic virtues. The common life, on the other hand, is useful in general for every- body, about which the patristic books tell us and teach us sufficiently. The spirit-speaking prophet David glorified it saying: "See now what is so good and so pleasant as for brethren to dwell together in unity!" (Ps. 133:1). In addition to this, one spirit-moved ecclesiastical hymn writes in this way: "Because in this the Lord promised eternal life." But also our good Master Lord God Jesus Christ, does he not say to us himself, by his immaculate lips: "Where two or three are gathered together in my name, there I am in the midst of them"? (Matt. 18:20). Our God-bearing fathers say for the solitary life: "Woe to him that is alone when he falls; and there is not a second to lift him up" (Eccl. 4:10)

Testament of St John of Rila – Page 133

" *Manual labor must not be neglected by you, however, but work must be in your hands, and the prayer "Lord Jesus Christ, Son of God, have mercy on me, a sinner" must be permanently on your lips, as well as the memory of death in your mind. This was the practice of the ancient desert fathers. They did not eat their bread in vain, and they not only lived themselves by labor of their own hands, but they gave to the needy too, and so they were not disappointed in their hope. "For," says the apostle [Paul], "it is well that the heart be strengthened by grace; not with foods which have not benefited their adherents" (Heb. 13:9). He says too: "Let brotherly love continue. Do not neglect to show hospitality to strangers; for thereby some have entertained angels unawares" (Heb. 13:1-2)."*

Testament of St John of Rila – Page 133

"I had much more to say to you, my beloved children in the Lord, but it is impossible to write everything. I deliver you to him who is the source of all wisdom and reason, and the true Comforter—to the Holy and life-giving Spirit, in order that he himself gives you wisdom, to bring you to your senses, to enlighten you, to teach and instruct you in every good deed."

My Experience with Ivan Rilski

In 2007 I went to Bulgaria, traveling to a friend I met in South Africa; running away from life's troubles seemed to make sense at that time!

The country of Bulgaria is simply beautiful, still recovering from their history like most of the Eastern Bloc countries. The Bulgarian people are friendly, social, and family-orientated. They love to spend time together and were very keen to help me get to know their country better.

My friends knowing, I was "religiously inclined", took me to some of the tourist places they knew would be of interest to me. The monastic communities all exist in beautiful wooded areas, away from the hustle and bustle of city life. In the wilderness, the heavy wooden structures were erected to deal with the cold Bulgarian winters and give the monks a place to encounter God on their terms, silence and serenity were their native tongue.

This was my first experience of Eastern Orthodox churches, walking inside the buildings the main altar looks completely different, with golden inlay into all the decorations, it feels like somebody discovered gold and decided this was a great decorative tool. Everything is guided in gold, with saints covering the heavy wooden walls, and icons painted on every panel, golden candle sticks and ceremonial golden bowls everywhere. I was a little taken aback by all the grandeur in such a hidden place.

I sat on my own, looking for a quiet corner, as all the faithful came to do their prayers for the day. I saw the gospel stories on the walls, painted for all those people who could not read or write in the Middle Ages.

Suddenly I could feel the love, the care, and the amount of labor this must have taken, I could feel the intentions of the painters, sculptors and monks, as they drew the gospels for the people, to give them some type of experience of God. And in this moment of awareness, I met Ivan Rilski.

This monastery was built close to the cave he made his home, for most of his life. I could feel his complete commitment to God, the fear of the Lord emanated from him and the serious nature of his walk with God. This was not a man you would trifle with, he had spent most of his life in the wild, the cold winters of Bulgaria made his will like iron; he loved God, and he would seek God, and nothing else would interrupt this task.

As I started choosing the saints, I felt Abba wanted to write about, John of Rila came quickly to mind. Few Christians in the West knew about this secret saint; the secret society of Bulgarian Christians with their well-worn clothes, seeking God in exceedingly difficult circumstances.

John spoke to me about the divine trinity of contemplation: solitude, silence, and rigorous repetition. He was careful to point out that mere silence of nature was not enough, silence of thought, and silence of desire was needed, only once we would come to the place where silence was complete could the voice of God speak to us, clearly, and unfettered by our human condition.

His desire for solitude was not for lack of love toward those monks around him; it was due to their loud thoughts and unending posturing that clamored for his attention – distracting him from the divine yearning for man.

I saw John sitting on a green moss-hewn rock, weekly giving instruction to the monks, yet admonishing them that the solitude made his words pure, he only kept the company of God and animals for in their voices he could hear the sound of the divine communicating the true way, the only way, prayer and supplication.

The rigorous repetition of the Jesus prayer, and other meditative prayers was his way of engaging with God. As the monks would come from time to time, he would then teach them about these revelations, often admonishing them, asking them why they received no revelation from the same books, and the same words, prayer and other methods they gave him. He saw in their hearts; the rigor of the practice, sometimes allowed them to escape into activity, using the monastic life and duties as an excuse for not searching the depths of the divine gaze.

John recounted to me that the hermetic and ascetic life is not for our generation, and that few would bare it. But a dedicated life, that is what we should seek. We should not wait for hours to be open in our schedule; we should find the minutes in the moments in between, and seek God in those moments, be rigorous not just in our practice, but also in our routine. The moments are there, and Jesus wants to fill them with visions, experiences and revelation that will sustain your walk.

It's easier than you think, but much harder when you live it, all intimacy in life is built on seeking time with God our Father. We become seekers, and then finding Him, we start seeking once more, the endless eternal rhythm of a relationship with God, that builds sons with a capacity of know the divine.

There is no vessel in the heart big enough to contain God, yet the heart of man is ever expanding in size, when focused on the attention of the loving Father, and knowing His Gaze. The eternal capacity that has been placed in the heart of man, is to build a place of timeless knowing, where the human heart is in constant communion, based only on the focused awareness of the gaze. The knowing in this place is not a knowing of information – it's a knowing of being.

We can only be at rest when we are not trying to answer questioners about God, or trying to beat our friend's revelations, but when we simply learn the ways of God. The ways, the thinking pattern of God, the Father is far less temporal, and much more focused on the divine expression of beauty in the human heart.

QUESTIONS

1. Which part of his life did you find thought provoking?
2. If you could write a testament to the people you leave behind, what would your instructions to them be?
3. If you could visit another church outside of your current denomination which would it be?
4. Do you think people in other parts of Christianity also pray to the same Jesus you are praying to, and what does this mean for our faith?

CHAPTER 5
Saint John of the Cross

"In the twilight of life, God will not judge us on our earthly possessions and human success, but rather on how much we have loved." – John of the Cross

Born:	1542
Died:	1591
Nationality:	Spain
Location:	Segovia Spain
Outlook:	Catholic Priest
Books:	Dark Night of the Soul Ascent of Mount Carmel Poems of St. John of the Cross
Interests:	Theology, Poetry
Achievements:	Doctor of the Church
Key Teachings:	Contemplative Life Process of awaking
Beatified:	25 January 1675
Canonized:	27 December 1726

The Life of Saint John of the Cross

John of the Cross (Juan de Yepes y Álvarez) was born at Fontiveros, Old Castile to a Messianic Jewish family in 1542. His father worked for their silk merchant family as a bookkeeper. Due to the death of his father and brother, his mother moved to Medina, where she could find more profitable work to provide for the family.

In Medina, he went to a school for orphans and the poor, also serving as an altar boy for the Augustan monastery. He worked at a local hospital while studying with the Jesuit collage from 1559 to 1563.

At the end of his studies, he joined the Carmelite order, and took a new name: John of St. Matthias. He then went on to study Theology and Philosophy at the Salamanca University.

John was ordained as a Priest in 1567. In Medina he met St. Terresa of Avilla who spoke to him about her reformation project, and restoring the Carmelite order to its former glory by keeping the "Primitive Rule"; a more strict rule that was not in practice at the time.

After completing his studies at Salamanca, John traveled with St. Terresa from Medina to Valladolid, where she was progressing in establishing a monastery.

Being convinced of her reforms, John established the first male monastery based on St. Terresa's principles on 28 November 1568, in an abandoned house given to St. Terresa of Avila. It was located in the town of Duruelo, close to Avila, with his companion Friar Antonio de Jesús de Heredia.

It was at this time that John also changed his name to John of the Cross. Due to their success, the house of friars became too small, leading the group to move to a town close by. Mancera de Abajo became the new place of their establishment.

John moved to another community at Pastrana in October 1570 and then onto Alcalá de Henares, to establish a theological training school for the friars and priests. St. Teressa of Avila became the prioress in Avila, and invited John to join her as spiritual director to the 130 nuns under her care, and the local community.

The reforms John and St. Terresa were advocating, caused an ecclesiastic split in the Carmelite order, between the "Discalced Houses", the houses and monasteries that reformed, and the normal Carmelite churches and communities.

The situation between the various parties deteriorated to such an extent that the Pope in Rome needed to intervene, however, the Spanish king supported the reforms of St. Terresa.

John was arrested and forced to move from Avila to Toledo, after being sentenced to imprisonment and multiple public whippings, he managed to escape his cell on 15 August 1578.

In 1579 he moved to Baeza to take the position of Rector at the Colegio de San Basilio, for Discalced friars in Andalusia. He stayed there until 1581, as a spiritual director and rector.

The Discalced Carmelites formally requested a separation from the Carmelite order, due to all the persecution they received. John of the Cross was elected as a leader of the group, and wrote the constitution for the new order after they received Papal sanction for the schism. At that time there were 22 houses, 300 friars and 200 nuns among the new Discalced Carmelites order.

In 1581 John was sent to help Ana de Jesus, establish a convent in Grenada. John stayed at the monastery of Los Mártires a short distance away. He became prior in 1582 to the monastery and learned of St. Theresa's death during 1582; his dear friend's loss was very troubling to him.

He traveled to Malaga in 1585, where he established a convent for the order. Later in the same year, John was elected as Vicar Provincial of Andalusia. The position required him to visit all those houses and friars under his care in the province.

Some estimate he traveled 25,000 km during his tenure. Considering that most of this travel was done by horse-drawn carriage, one can only imagine the physical and mental toll this might have been for him.

In 1588 he was elected as Councilor to the Vicar General for the Discalced Carmelites. To take this role he needed to move to Segovia in Castile, where he also served as the prior to the local monastery.

After a disagreement over reforms with Father Nicolas Doria, a leader in the order after St. Theresa's death, he was transferred to La Peñuela, an isolated monastery in Andalusia.

He became sick at the monastery and sought medical treatment at the monastery at Úbeda, where he died on 4 December 1591 from a medical condition called "erysipelas."

The Doctrine of Saint John of the Cross

"To love is to be transformed into what we love. To love God is therefore to be transformed into God."

John of the Cross

The Dark Night of the Soul separates the dark night into 3 major timeframes:

a) The Dusk

b) Deep Night

c) Dawn

The three timeframes describe the different periods of the dark night, and how the child of God progresses along the path of progression towards awakening from the dark night, into a place of conscious understanding.

Dark Night of the Soul – Page 20, Behavior of Spiritually Immature

Sometimes, too, when their spiritual masters, such as confessors and superiors, do not approve of their spirit and behavior (for they are anxious that all they do shall be esteemed and praised), they consider that they do not understand them, or that, because they do not approve of this and comply with that, their confessors are themselves not spiritual. And so they immediately desire and contrive to find some one else who will fit in with their tastes; for as a rule they desire to speak of spiritual matters with those who they think will praise and esteem what they do, and they flee, as they would from death, from those who disabuse them in order to lead them into a safe road—sometimes they even harbour ill-will against them.

Dark Night of the Soul – Page 22, Constant Spiritual Seeking

Many of these beginners have also at times great spiritual avarice. They will be found to be discontented with the spirituality which God gives them; and they are very disconsolate and querulous because they find not in spiritual things the consolation that they would desire. Many can never have enough of listening to counsels and learning spiritual precepts, and of possessing and reading many books which treat of this matter, and they spend their time on all these things rather than on works of mortification and the perfecting of the inward poverty of spirit which should be theirs.

Dark Night of the Soul – Page 32, The Start of the Dark Night

God turns all this light of theirs into darkness, and shuts against them the door and the source of the sweet spiritual water which they were tasting in God whensoever and for as long as they desired. (For, as they were weak and tender, there was no door closed to them, as Saint John says in the Apocalypse, iii, 8). And thus He leaves them so completely in the dark that they know not whither to go with their sensible imagination and meditation; for they cannot advance a step in meditation, as they were wont to do afore time, their inward senses being submerged in this night, and left with such dryness that not only do they experience no pleasure and consolation in the spiritual things and good exercises wherein they were wont to find their delights and pleasures, but instead, on the contrary, they find insipidity and bitterness in the said things.

Dark Night of the Soul – Page 34, The Wilderness of the Growing Believer

These souls whom God is beginning to lead through these solitary places of the wilderness are like to the children of Israel, to whom in the wilderness God began to give food from Heaven, containing within itself all sweetness, and, as is there said, it turned to the savour which each one of them desired. But withal the children of Israel felt the lack of the pleasures and delights of the flesh and the onions which they had eaten aforetime in Egypt, the more so because their palate was accustomed to these and took delight in them, rather than in the delicate sweetness of the angelic manna; and they wept and sighed for the fleshpots even in the midst of the food of Heaven

Dark Night of the Soul – Page 42, The Path of Spiritual Humility

Likewise, from the aridities and voids of this night of the desire, the soul draws spiritual humility, which is the contrary virtue to the first capital sin, which, as we said, is spiritual pride. Through this humility, which is acquired by the said knowledge of self, the soul is purged from all those imperfections where into it fell with respect to that sin of pride, in the time of its prosperity. For it sees itself so dry and miserable that the idea never even occurs to it that it is making better progress than others, or outstripping them, as it believed itself to be doing before. On the contrary, it recognizes that others are making better progress than itself.

Dark Night of the Soul – Page 56, The Divine Cleansing the Spiritual "Soul"

The Divine assails the soul in order to renew it and thus to make it Divine;

and, stripping it of the habitual affections and attachments of the old man, to which it is very closely united, knit together and conformed, destroys and consumes its spiritual substance, and absorbs it in deep and profound darkness. As a result of this, the soul feels itself to be perishing and melting away, in the presence and sight of its miseries, in a cruel spiritual death, even as if it had been swallowed by a beast and felt itself being devoured in the darkness of its belly, suffering such anguish as was endured by Jonas in the belly of that beast of the sea.116 For in this sepulcher of dark death it must needs abide until the spiritual resurrection which it hopes for.

Dark Night of the Soul – Page 66, Promise of Divine Union

Divine, and therefore very spiritual, subtle and delicate, and very 'with a certain eminence of excellence. 'sweetness, with great eminence. Intimate, transcending every affection and feeling of the will, and every desire thereof, it is fitting that, in order that the will may be able to attain to this Divine affection and most lofty delight, and to feel it and experience it through the union of love, since it is not, in the way of nature, perceptible to the will, it be first of all purged and annihilated in all its affections and feelings, and left in a condition of aridity and constraint, proportionate to the habit of natural affections which it had before, with respect both to Divine things and to human.

Dark Night of the Soul – Page 73

This is one kind of suffering which proceeds from this dark night; but, he goes on to say, with my spirit, in my bowels, until the morning, I will watch for Thee. And this is the second way of grieving in desire and yearning which comes from love in the bowels of the spirit, which are the spiritual affections. But in the midst of these dark and loving afflictions the soul feels within itself a certain companionship and strength, which bears it company and so greatly strengthens it that, if this burden of grievous darkness be taken away, it often feels itself to be alone, empty and weak. The cause of this is that, as the strength and efficacy of the soul were derived and communicated passively from the dark fire of love which assailed it, it follows that, when that fire ceases to assail it, the darkness and power and heat of love cease in the soul.

Dark Night of the Soul – Page 84, Spiritual Soul

Therefore, O spiritual soul, when thou seest thy desire obscured, thy affections arid and constrained, and thy faculties bereft of their capacity for any interior exercise, be not afflicted by this, but rather consider it a great happiness, since God is freeing thee from thyself and taking the matter from thy hands. For with those hands, howsoever well they may serve thee, thou wouldst never labour so effectively, so perfectly and so securely (because of their clumsiness and uncleanness) as now, when God takes thy hand and guides thee in the darkness, as though thou wert blind, to an end and by a way which thou knowest not. Nor couldst thou ever hope to travel with the aid of thine own eyes and feet, howsoever good thou be as a walker.

Dark Night of the Soul – Page 95, Not Letting Go

The eighth step of love causes the soul to seize Him and hold Him fast without letting Him go, even as the Bride says, after this manner: 'I found Him Whom my heart and soul love; I held Him and I will not let Him go.'257 On this step of union the soul satisfies her desire, but not continuously. Certain souls climb some way,258 and then lose their hold; for, if this state were to continue, it would be glory itself in this life; and thus the soul remains therein for very short periods of time. To the prophet Daniel, because he was a man of desires, was sent a command from God to remain on this step, when it was said to him: 'Daniel, stay upon thy step, because thou art a man of desires.'259 After this step follows the ninth, which is that of souls now perfect, as we shall afterwards say, which is that that follows.

Ascent of Mount Carmel – Page 58, Summary of the Seasons of the Night

These three parts of the night are all one night; but, after the manner of night, it has three parts. For the first part, which is that of sense, is comparable to the beginning of night, the point at which things begin to fade from sight. And the second part, which is faith, is comparable to midnight, which is total darkness. And the third part is like the close of night, which is God, the which part is now near to the light of day. And, that we may understand this the better, we shall treat of each of these reasons separately as we proceed.

Ascent of Mount Carmel – Page 62, Wisdom in Man's Eyes

All the wisdom of the world and all human ability, compared with the infinite wisdom of God, are pure and supreme ignorance, even as Saint Paul writes ad Corinthios, saying: Sapientia hujus mundi stultitia est apud Deum.95 'The wisdom of this world is foolishness with God.' Wherefore any soul that makes account of all its knowledge and ability in order to come to union with the wisdom of God is supremely ignorant in the eyes of God and will remain far removed from that wisdom; for ignorance knows not what wisdom is, even as Saint Paul says that this wisdom seems foolishness to God; since, in the eyes of God, those who consider themselves to be persons with a certain amount of knowledge are very ignorant

Ascent of Mount Carmel – Page 62, Faith in the Dark Night Grows

So that which is to be inferred from this that faith, because it is dark night, gives light to the soul, which is in darkness, that there may come to be fulfilled that which David likewise says to this purpose, in these works: Et nox illuminatio mea in deliciis meis.224 Which signifies: the night will be illumination in my delights. Which is as much as to say: In the delights of my pure contemplation and union with God, the night of faith shall be my guide. Wherein he gives it clearly to be understood that the soul must be in darkness in order to have light for this road.

Ascent of Mount Carmel – Page 192, Divine Action upon the Soul

And, although it is true that hardly any soul will be found that is moved by God in all things and at all times, and has such continual union with God that, without the mediation of any form, its faculties are ever moved divinely, there are nevertheless souls who in their operations are very habitually moved by God, and these are not they that are moved of themselves, for, as Saint Paul says, the sons of God who are transformed and united in God, are moved by the Spirit of God,488 that is, are moved to perform Divine work in their faculties. And it is no marvel that their operations should be Divine, since the union of the soul is Divine.

Ascent of Mount Carmel – Page 250, Meditation and Conversation with God.

WITH regard to the direction of the spirit to God through this kind of good, it is well to point out that it is certainly lawful, and even expedient, for beginners to find some sensible sweetness and pleasure in images, oratories and other visible objects of devotion, since they have not yet weaned or detached their desire670 from things of the world, so that they can leave the one pleasure for the other. They are like a child holding something in one of its hands; to make it loosen its hold upon it we give it something else to hold in the other hand lest it should cry because both its hands are empty. But the spiritual person that would make progress must strip himself of all those pleasures and desires wherein the will can rejoice, for pure spirituality is bound very little to any of those objects, but only to interior recollection and mental converse with God.

My Journey with Saint John of the Cross

The first time I encountered John of the Cross was while on "pilgrimage" to Santiago de Compostela, not the usual way of walking or riding a bike, but nonetheless purposefully visiting the old town surrounded by the beautiful and historic buildings. Ending my time there attending the weekly Mass for the Pilgrims.

During my stay I saw in a vision how John writing with his finger in the sand; he drew a few pathways and started explaining the journey into intimacy with God. He explained the cadence of the pilgrim, how every step is a reminder of the way of life, how one can walk the Camino in a conscious way, not just honoring the Saints who have walked this path before, but also walking in step with Jesus our Master.

As he talked, I saw his feet, matching the feet of Jesus, how he had taught himself never to walk slower or faster than the Master. I realized John knew how to be in lockstep with Jesus, he understood the unforced rhythms of grace, like a metronome their feet synchronized. Next to them, my walking was like a drunkard with a broken leg!

I got very frustrated with the process, and then, Jesus started dancing, grabbed my arms and started laughing with me, and saying, "son it takes time, relax, enjoy the journey, you will reach mastery if you learn to enjoy before you try to master."

John then showed me how he gently pulled the strands of his robe and one by one the strands started to unravel the whole robe from the bottom upwards. "Friend, if you are able to start to pull at and remove even a few small strands of your old spiritual habits, and release all the old ways you used to use to calm your heart and believe that you are pleasing God, at one stage the cloth of religion will come undone. This is the path of spiritual growth, to allow the nakedness of your own ability, to become a new garment of joy and praise."

In the vision, John's "new" robe started to have colorful strands, he explained that the strands were the places he lived on earth and allowed God to fully use his life, to do the divine will. Our life on earth is built on these small moments, becoming a spiritual tapestry of patterns on our spiritual clothes.

Our ideas of spiritual growth and our thoughts on building virtues in our own lives almost seemed like self-help books or motivational physiology, instead of learning to listen to the voice of the Master Jesus Christ. If we were to become the Church that Christ intended, we need to become spiritual guides to those in our care.

As they share their experiences and scriptural understanding, we should simply enjoy their growth, and not try to force them into the same models and frameworks of "Mega-church" and "Church Growth" models. Love them onto the place that God has called them into.

The church of the future would value conversation and preaching on the same level, in the visions he showed me how they would conduct what was called in their era "Spiritual direction" and how much we have neglected this process for the sake of administration and physiological approaches.

A retuning to the King of the Kingdom, who values participation more than just exposition of scripture, living epistles of change.

While researching for the book, I read the Dank Night of the Soul and during one time of meditation, I asked why the dark night is needed, and why the process of suffering is needed.

The answer came softly, "Unless a seed falls to the ground and dies..."; John explained the process of germination for a seed, the process of death and life in that moment. How a seed can only become what it is destined for a fully fruitful plant, able to reproduce and produce a seed of its own.

This place of death in the process of germinating is the process of the dark night. This is where the soul is taught to walk by inner reality, not outer circumstances, or any normal light. This place of dying, this reality of reconfiguration, resets the heart to see into the dimensions and realms of divinity, devoid of the imaginations, stripped bare from the skins or masks of the part, the reality of divinity, starts invading the realm of the individual whom no longer is only an individual, but has become part of the One.

QUESTIONS

1. Which part of his life intrigued you the most?

2. From the Extract of "Dark night of the Soul" which part did you enjoy the most and why?

3. Do you think this dark night of the soul is needed for every Christian?

4. If you have ever experienced a hard season in your walk with God, what helped you move on to the next season in the past?

5. What shortens the process of suffering in our lives the most?

CHAPTER 6
Saint Dominic Guzman

"Heretics are to be converted by an example of humility and other virtues far more readily than by any external display or verbal battles. So let us arm ourselves with devout prayers and set off showing signs of genuine humility and go barefooted to combat Goliath." – Saint Dominic

CHAPTER 6 - Saint Dominic Guzman

Born:	8 August 1170
Died:	6 August 1221
Nationality:	Spain
Location:	Rome, Italy
Outlook:	Dominican
Achievements:	Doctor of the Church
Key Teachings:	Care for the Poor, Teaching the Rosary
Supernatural Miracles:	Working with Angels, Healings, miracles, signs and wonders
Canonized:	29 June 1461

The Life of Saint Dominic

Saint Dominic was born in Caleruega in Spain on the 8th of August 1170 to Felix de Guzman and Jane of Aza. His parents were wealthy pillars of the community.

Dominic went to school in Palencia where he studied the arts for 6 years, and then studied 4 years in the field of Theology. In 1194 at the age of 25, he became part of the Canons Regular at the Cathedral of Osma, following the rule of Saint Augustine in the community of the monastery.

In 1204 he joined a diplomatic mission with Diego de Acebo, the Bishop of Osma, for the king of Spain (Castile) Alonso VIII, to arrange a bride in Denmark for Prince Ferdinand. The marriage was arranged, however, the princes of Denmark died en route to Spain.

In 1205, Dominic and Diego de Acebo started an evangelistic campaign to convert the Cathars in the South of France. This group was seen as heretics by the Catholic Church due to their Gnostic Theological ideas. Their work did not progress well, and was halted, due to the Cathars' resistance to their message.

Dominic saw the changing culture in the cities during 1215 and the requirement for changes to the spiritual needs of society. He started with a system based on education, and flexible rules for monastics and laity who desired spiritual direction. Bishop Foulques gave him permission to preach and teach in the Toulouse region.

Later in the same year, Dominic went to Rome to obtain a Papal sanction. The "Order of Preachers" was formed which later became the Dominican order, after they received Papal approval.

The Pope Honorius III invited Dominic to Rome, where he made the city the headquarters for his newly established order at Santa Sabina, now known as the "Mother Church of the Dominicans."

Dominic then went to Bologna in 1218 where he lived at the church of San Nicolò of the Vineyards. Some of his companions started a convent in the same area. This became the same place where the first meetings of the

Dominican orders were held.

Dominic then traveled to St Nicholas at Bologna, Italy, where he died on the 6th of August 1221, at the age of 51.

Theology of Saint Dominic

"To read, joy; to think, delight; to write, torture." **Saint Dominic**

Although Saint Dominic did not write many works, his preaching and lifestyle was his method of changing the world. He truly lived a life where actions spoke louder than words.

Below are some extracts from his letters, written by his own hand, and other works dictated to his scribes. Also included below are some of the miracle stories of his life. Although not formally captured, his life speaks volumes of theology, not in an intellectual way, but as a lived reality.

Changing the world, step by step, sermon by sermon, living the example of Christ to others. To quote St Francis of Assisi *"Preach the Gospel at all times. When necessary, use words."*; it seems both these men where reading from the same hymn sheet.

The nine ways of prayer summarized below, were written by an unknown author, however, probably written by Sister Cecilia of the monastery of St. Agnes at Bologna who knew Dominic personally and received her nun's habit from him directly.

The Dominican way of prayer is based on the movement of the body, which Dominic believed had an impact on the soul, in essence, the whole person is praying not just the vocal sounds from the disciple of Christ, but his whole attitude to prayer.

Nine Ways of Prayer – St Dominic

1) Bowing Deeply

"First of all, bowing humbly before the altar as if Christ, whom the altar signifies, were really and personally present and not just symbolically. As it says, 'The prayer of the person who humbles himself will pierce the clouds' (Ecclus. 35:21). He used sometimes to say to the brethren the text from Judith, 'The prayer of the humble and meek has always been pleasing to you' (Judith 9:16). It was by humility that the Canaanite woman obtained what she wanted (Matt. 15:22-28), and so did the prodigal son (Luke 15:18-24). Also, 'I am not worthy to have you come under my roof' (Matt. 8:8). 'Lord, humble my spirit deeply because, Lord, I am utterly humbled before you' (Ecclus. 7:19; Psalms 118). So the holy father, standing with his body erect, would bow his head and his heart humbly before Christ his Head, considering his own servile condition and the outstanding nobility of Christ, and giving himself up entirely to venerating him.

He taught the brethren to do this whenever they passed before a crucifix showing the humiliation of Christ, so that Christ, who was humbled for our sake, might particularly see us humbled before his greatness. Similarly he told the brethren to humble themselves like this before the whole Trinity whenever 'Glory be to the Father and to the Son and to the Holy Spirit' was recited solemnly. This way of prayer was the beginning of his devotion: bowing deeply."

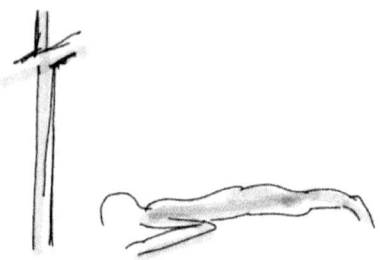

2) Flat Prostration on the Ground

St. Dominic also often used to pray throwing himself down on the ground, flat on his face, and then his heart would be pricked with compunction and he would blush at himself and say, sometimes loudly enough for it actually to be heard, the words from the gospel, 'Lord, be merciful to me, a sinner' (Luke 18:13). And with great devotion and reverence he would recite the words of David, 'It is I who have sinned and done unjustly' (2 Sam. 24:17). He would weep and groan passionately and then say, 'I am not worthy to look upon the height of heaven, because of the greatness of my sin; I have provoked your anger and done evil in your sight' (Prayer of Manasseh 9-10). He would also say, emphatically and devoutly, the verse from Psalm 43:25, 'My soul is laid low in the dust, my belly is stuck to the earth.' And again, 'My soul is stuck to the floor, make me come alive according to your word' (Ps. 118:25).

Sometimes, wanting to teach the brethren with what reverence they ought to pray, he would say to them, 'The Magi, those devout kings, entered the house and found the child with Mary, his mother (Matt. 2:11). Now it is certain that we have found him too. God and man, with Mary his handmaid, so come, let us fall down and worship before God, let us weep before the Lord who made us' (Ps. 94:6).

He exhorted the young men too, saying to them, 'If you cannot weep for your own sins, because you have none, still there are many sinners to be directed towards mercy and love, for whose sake the prophets and apostles groaned in distress, and for their sake too Jesus wept bitterly when he saw them (Luke 19:41), and similarly the holy David wept and said, "I saw the half-hearted and I pined away"' (Ps. 118:158).

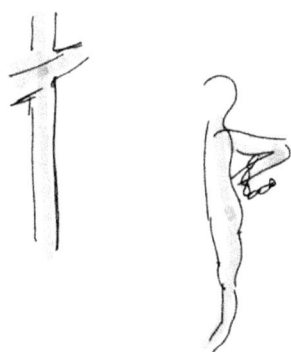

3) Pain and Suffering of Prayer

*"For this reason, rising up from the ground, he used to take the discipline with an iron chain saying, 'Your discipline has set me straight towards my goal' (Ps. 17:36). This is why the whole order determined that all the brethren, out of respect for the memory of St. Dominic's example, should take the discipline on their bare backs with sticks of wood every ferial day after Compline, saying the **Miserere or the De profundis**. They were to do this either for their own sins or for those of others whose gifts support them. So no one, however innocent, should withdraw himself from following this holy example.*

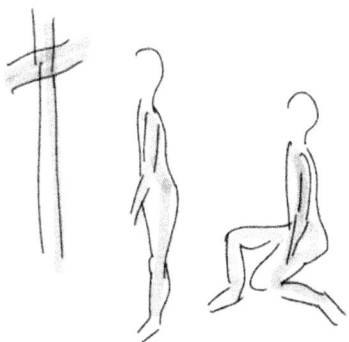

4) The Fixating Gaze on Jesus

After this, St. Dominic, standing before the altar or in the chapter room, would fix his gaze on the crucifix, looking intently at Christ on the cross and kneeling down over and over again, a hundred times perhaps; sometimes he would even spend the whole time from after Compline until midnight getting up and kneeling down again, like the apostle James, and like the leper in the gospel who knelt down and said, 'Lord, if you will you can make me clean' (Mark 1:40), and like Stephen who knelt down and cried out with a loud voice, 'Lord, do not hold this sin against them' (Acts 7:59). And a great confidence would grow in our holy father Dominic, confidence in God's mercy for himself and for all sinners, and for the protection of the novices whom he used to send out all over the place to preach to souls. And sometimes he could not contain his voice, but the brethren would hear him saying, 'To you, Lord, I will cry, do not turn away from me in silence, lest in your silence I become like those who go down into the pit' (Ps. 27:1), and other such words from sacred scripture.

At other times, however, he spoke in his heart and his voice was not heard at all (1 Sam.1:13), and he would remain quietly on his knees, his mind caught up in wonder, and this sometimes lasted a long time. Sometimes it seemed from the very way he looked that he had penetrated heaven in his mind, and then he would suddenly appear radiant with joy, wiping away the abundant tears running down his face. At such times he would come to be in an intensity of desire, like a thirsty man coming to a spring of water (Ecclus. 26:15), or a traveler at last approaching his own country. Then he would grow more forceful and insistent, and his movements would display great composure and agility as he stood up and knelt down.

He was so accustomed to genuflecting that, when he was on a journey, whether in a hostel after the toils of the road or on the road itself, while the others were sleeping or resting, he would return to his genuflections as to his own special art and his own personal service. This way of prayer he taught more by the example of his practice than by what he said.

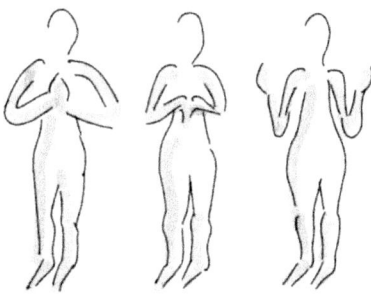

5)   Open Hands Receiving Position – Clasped Hands

Sometimes, when he was in a priory, our holy father Dominic would stand upright before the altar, not leaning on anything or supported by anything, but with his whole body standing erect on his feet. Sometimes he would hold his hands out, open, before his breast, like an open book, and then he would stand with great reverence and devotion, as if he were reading in the presence of God. At such times he seemed to be meditating, savoring the words of God in his mouth and, as it were, enjoying reciting them to himself. He had made his own the Lord's practice which we read about in Luke 4:16, 'Jesus went into the synagogue on the Sabbath day, as it was his custom to do, and stood up to read.' And it says in Psalm 105:30, 'Phineas stood and prayed and the pestilence stopped.'

At other times he joined his hands and held them tightly fastened together in front of his eyes, hunching himself up. At other times he raised his hands to his shoulders, in the manner of a priest saying Mass, as if he wanted to fix his ears more attentively on something that was being said to him by someone else. If you had seen his devotion as he stood there, erect in prayer, you would have thought you were looking at a prophet conversing with an angel or with God, now talking, now listening, now thinking quietly about what had been revealed to him.

When he was travelling, he would steal sudden moments of prayer, unobtrusively, and would stand with his whole mind instantaneously concentrated on heaven, and soon you would have heard him pronouncing, with the utmost enjoyment and relish, some lovely text from the very heart of sacred scripture, which he would seem to have drawn fresh from the Savior's wells (Is. 12:3).

> *The brethren used to be greatly moved by this example, when they saw their father and master praying in this way, and the more devout among them found it the best possible instruction in how to pray continuously*

and reverently, 'as the eyes of a handmaid are on the hands of her mistress and as the eyes of servants are on the hands of their masters' (Ps. 122:2).

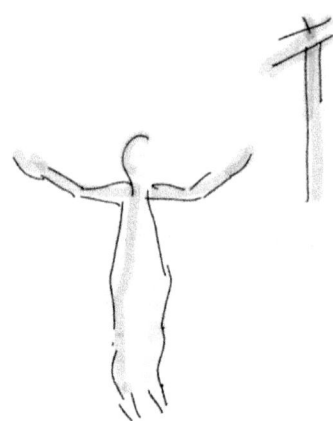

6) Hands Stretched Out and Crucifix Position

Sometimes, when he was in a priory, our holy father Dominic would stand upright before the altar, not leaning on anything or supported by anything, but with his whole body standing erect on his feet. Sometimes he would hold his hands out, open, before his breast, like an open book, and then he would stand with great reverence and devotion, as if he were reading in the presence of God. At such times he seemed to be meditating, savoring the words of God in his mouth and, as it were, enjoying reciting them to himself. He had made his own the Lord's practice which we read about in Luke 4:16, 'Jesus went into the synagogue on the Sabbath day, as it was his custom to do, and stood up to read.' And it says in Psalm 105:30, 'Phineas stood and prayed and the pestilence stopped.'

At other times he joined his hands and held them tightly fastened together in front of his eyes, hunching himself up. At other times he raised his hands to his shoulders, in the manner of a priest saying Mass, as if he wanted to fix his ears more attentively on something that was being said to him by someone else. If you had seen his devotion as he stood there, erect in prayer, you would have thought you were looking at a prophet conversing with an angel or with God, now talking, now listening, now thinking quietly about what had been revealed to him.

When he was travelling, he would steal sudden moments of prayer, unobtrusively, and would stand with his whole mind instantaneously concentrated on heaven, and soon you would have heard him pronouncing, with the utmost enjoyment and relish, some lovely text from the very heart of sacred scripture, which he would seem to have drawn fresh from the Savior's wells (Is. 12:3).

The brethren used to be greatly moved by this example, when they saw their father and master praying in this way, and the more devout among them found it the best possible instruction in how to pray continuously and reverently, 'as the eyes of a handmaid are on the hands of her mistress and as the eyes of servants are on the hands of their masters' (Ps. 122:2).

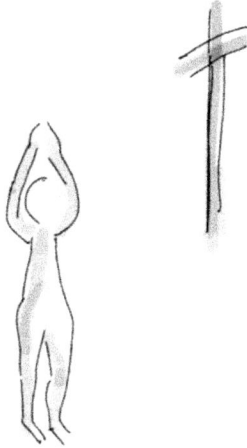

7) Arms stretched out before you – like an arrow – whole body position or just arms

He was also often found stretching his whole body up towards heaven in prayer, like a choice arrow shot straight up from a bow (Is. 49:2). He had his hands stretched right up above his head, joined together or slightly open as if to catch something from heaven. And it is believed that at such times he received an increase of grace and was caught up in rapture, and that his prayer won from God, for the order he had founded, the gifts of the Holy Spirit and, for himself and for his brethren, such delight and enjoyment in putting the Beatitudes into practice that each one would consider himself blessed in the most profound poverty, in bitter grief, in severe persecution, in great hunger and thirst for righteousness, in all the cares and worries of mercy (Matt. 5:3-10), and that they would all consider it a pleasure to observe the commandments with devotion and to follow the evangelical counsels. At such times the holy father seemed suddenly to enter the Holy of Holies and the third heaven (2 Cor. 12:2). And so, after this kind of prayer, he bore himself like a prophet, as is related in his miracles, whether he was rebuking or dispensing or preaching. Just one example must be given here, briefly, for edification's sake.

Once at Bologna, after praying like this, the holy master Dominic asked the advice of some of the senior brethren about some decision that had to be made. This was his normal practice because, as he said, something may be shown to one good man which is not shown to another, as can be seen in the prophets. The sacristan then came and called one of the people taking part in this council to go to the women's church, to hear a confession, I think. He added, stupidly, though not, as he thought, loudly enough to be heard by the holy master Dominic, 'A beautiful lady is asking for you; come at once.' Then the Spirit came upon St. Dominic and he began to be disturbed in himself, and the councilors looked at him with fear. Then he told the sacristan to come to him and he asked him, 'What did you say?' He replied, 'I was asking for a priest to come to the church.' And the father said, 'Reproach yourself and confess the sin which came to your lips. The God who made all things made me aware of what you thought were your secret words.' And he disciplined him there severely and long, so that those who were present were moved to compassion because of his bruises. Then he said, 'Go, my son; now you have learned how to gaze at a woman in the future. Make sure you do not judge of her appearance. And you too should pray that God will give you chaste eyes.' In this way he knew what was hidden, rebuked the brother's folly and punished him and taught him, as he had foreseen it all in prayer. And the brethren were amazed that this was what he said had to be done. And the holy master said, 'All our justice, by comparison with that of God, is nothing better than filth' (Is. 64:6).

So the holy father did not remain long in this kind of prayer, but returned to himself as if he were coming from far away, and at such times he seemed to be a stranger in the world, as could easily be seen from his appearance and his behavior. While he was praying he was sometimes clearly heard by the brethren saying, as the prophet did, 'Hear the voice of my supplication while I pray to you and while I lift up my hands to your holy temple' (Ps. 27:2). And the holy master taught the brethren to pray like this, both by his words and by his example. He quoted from Psalm 133:2, 'At night lift up your hands to the holy place,' and Psalm 140:2, 'The raising of my hands like an evening sacrifice.'

8) Seated and alert position

The holy father Dominic also had another beautiful way of praying, full of devotion and grace. After the canonical hours and the grace which is said in common after meals the father would go off quickly to some place where he could be alone, in a cell or somewhere. Sober and alert and anointed with a spirit of devotion which he had drawn from the words of God which had been sung in choir or during the meal, he would settle himself down to read or pray, recollecting himself in himself and fixing himself in the presence of God. Sitting there quietly, he would open some book before him, arming himself first with the sign of the cross, and then he would read. And he would be moved in his mind as delightfully as if he heard the Lord speaking to him. As the Psalm says, 'I will hear what the Lord God is saying in me, because he will speak peace to his people and upon his saints, and to those who turn to him with all their heart' (Ps. 84:9). It was as if he were arguing with a friend; at one moment he would appear to be feeling impatient, nodding his head energetically, then he would seem to be listening quietly, then you would see him disputing and struggling, and laughing and weeping all at once, fixing then lowering his gaze, then again speaking quietly and beating his breast. If anyone was inquisitive enough to want to spy on him secretly, he would find that the holy father Dominic was like Moses, who went into the innermost desert and saw the burning bush and the Lord speaking and calling to him to humble himself (Exod. 3:1ff). The man of God had a prophetic way of passing over quickly from reading to prayer and from meditation to contemplation.

When he was reading like this on his own, he used to venerate the book and bow to it and sometimes kiss it, particularly if it was a book of the gospels or if he was reading the words which Christ had spoken with his own lips. And sometimes he used to hide his face and turn it aside, or he would bury his face in his hands or hide it a little in his scapular. And then he would also become anxious and full of yearning, and he would also rise a little, respectfully, and bow as if he were thanking some very special person for favors received. Then, quite refreshed and at peace in himself, he would continue reading his book.

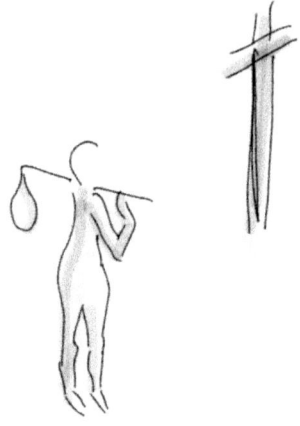

9) The lingering prayer – meditative jaunt

He also used to observe this way of prayer when he was going from one country to another, especially when he was in a lonely place. He disported himself with his meditations in his contemplation. And sometimes he would say to his travelling companions, 'It is written in Hosea, "I will lead her to a lonely place and speak to her heart"' (Hos. 2:14). So sometimes he went aside from his companion or went on ahead or, more likely, lingered far behind; going on his own he would pray as he walked, and a fire was kindled in his meditation (Ps. 38:4).

A curious thing about this kind of prayer was that he seemed to be brushing away ashes or flies from his face, and because of this he often defended himself with the sign of the cross. The brethren thought that in this kind of prayer the saint acquired the fullness of sacred scripture and the very heart of the understanding of God's words, and also a power and boldness to preach fervently and a hidden intimacy with the Holy Spirit to know hidden things.

Thus it happened once, to mention just one story out of many which we omit, that the devil came to the church of the Friars Preachers in Bologna in the form of a young man of frivolous, licentious character and asked for someone to hear his confession. Five priests were brought to him, one after another. This was because the first confessor was so viciously disturbed and enflamed by his words that he got up from listening to his confession and refused to hear such dreadful things to the end. The second did the same and so did the third, fourth and fifth. But they went away without saying anything and they were not prepared to reveal this confession because, as far as they were concerned, what they had heard was a sacramental confession, even though it was the devil's. Then the sacristan approached St. Dominic, who was in the priory at the time, complaining about these priests, because five of them had not been able to hear one sinner's confession. 'It's scandalous,' he added, 'the priests preach penance and then they refuse to give a penance to sinners.' Then the holy father Dominic got up from his reading and prayer and contemplation, not, I think, unaware of what was afoot, and went to hear the devil's confession. When he entered the church, the devil came to him and at once the holy father recognized him and said to him, 'You evil spirit, why do you tempt the servants of God under this veil of piety?' And he rebuked him severely. The devil disappeared at once, leaving the church reeking of sulfur. And the sacristan was appeased and stopped being angry with the priests.

Miracles and Visions by Dominic

Dominic Receives the Rosary from Mary Mother of Jesus

One night in 1208, while St. Dominic was hard at prayer in the Chapel of Notre Dame de la Prouille, [13]Our Lady appeared to him. Holding the Rosary, She said, "Be of good courage, Dominic; the fruits of your labor shall be abundant. The remedy for the evils which you lament will be meditation on the life, death and glory of my Son, uniting thereto the recitation of the Angelic Salutation (Hail Mary) by which the mystery of redemption was announced to the world. "This devotion you are to inculcate by your preaching, is a practice most dear to my Son and to me - as a most powerful means of dissipating heresy, extinguishing vice, propagating virtue, imploring divine mercy, and obtaining my protection. I desire that not only you, but all those who shall enter your Order, perpetually promote this manner of prayer. The faithful will obtain by it innumerable advantages and will always find me ready to aid them in their wants. This is the precious gift which I leave to you and to your spiritual children.

The miracle of the bread and the wine of Angels – Page 26

One day the brothers had been unsuccessfully begging for alms all day and were dejectedly returning to the convent when they met up with a woman. Feeling compassion on them, she gave them a loaf of bread. They walked a few steps when they were stopped by a poor man begging; he asked them for their loaf of bread. They, at first, insisted that it was all they had, but upon his persisting pleading turned the bread over to him. Now, while this was happening, the Lord had enlightened St. Dominic what had come to pass, so when the brothers approached he asked them if they had returned with nothing! When they recounted what had transpired, he said, "Have no fear; it was an Angel of the Lord."

Dominic summoned the whole community to come and eat in the refectory. He insisted, over their protests, they prepare the tables for their nightly meal. They were all seated; Dominic gave the blessing and one of the brothers began to read, aloud. Dominic prayed! Suddenly two handsome young men appeared and began distributing bread. After the last loaf was dispensed, they disappeared. Then Dominic instructed the community to eat the bread the Lord had provided. Dominic then charged the brothers to pour the wine; and when they said there was none, he insisted they obey him, take the vessels and pour the wine which the Lord has provided. They obeyed and they not only filled all the glasses, they had enough wine and bread for three days! The third day, Dominic instructed them to keep none, but give the rest to the poor.

Dominic's vision of Jesus in Heaven with Mother Mary

Dominic went off to pray and suddenly he went into ecstasy and had a vision of Jesus with the Blessed Mother standing on His right; looking around he saw every Order but his standing before the throne of God. He began to weep, as if his heart would break; the Lord asked him why he wept; to which Dominic replied, "I weep because I see every Order before You but mine." The Lord said that that was because He had entrusted his Order to His Mother. Then when the Lord asked him if he desired to see his Order, Mother Mary opened her mantle wide so that it covered all the heavens and underneath were friars extending beyond where the eye could see. With that he awakened from his ecstasy; he called the friars to prayer and began instructing them on the love and veneration owed to the Mother of God, Mary most holy.

Personal Experience of Saint Dominic

In a vision Dominic walked up to me with bread in his hands, saying: "Before we spend any time together, we need to first have communion together; there can be no common union between us, if we don't share in the common union of Christ Jesus, in the Body of His, divine resurrection."

Dominic considered prayer of the body hugely important and made much effort with every position and every movement; methodically teaching it to all the saints, not by preaching, but by acting, by living, by showing and assuming they would follow his example if, according to him, his life was deemed worthy of their attention.

Every moment of the body creates a movement of the heart, once bowed down low, it is hard for the heart of man to be full of pride when one is laid down prostrate before the Lord. The heart of man, although "evil and deceitful in every way", can be trained by constant practice of the body to accept the Lordship of the Master by constant attention.

The movement of the body helps the heart and mind focus on holding the position, and thus keeping the attention on the action of the disciple. It is sometimes easier to train the body in constant concentration than forcing a wondering mind or an emotional heart to move in the same coherent direction. The body however is trained by memory, the muscle of practice, creates a habit of focus, which can be used to focus the rest of the faculties on the divine – while the rebellion in the soul remains.

Dominic sternly warned against outward actions but with inward waywardness, this will lead to the enactment of divine virtue, and the inner thoughts being viler than before, seeking the attention of man, and the praise of men, makes the exercises of the body in worship as useless as dry bones.

The body is only able to align a heart disposed to worship, prayer and the beautiful gaze of the beloved Jesus. Outward actions might teach one to focus, however, without a heart consecrated and set on the virtue of the Christ, mere discipline will not bear fruits of repentance.

Just as the seven Hebrew words for praise and worship have actions linked to them, the nine ways of prayer, have also been linked to different versions of the liturgy and can be used to memorize the scriptures, build prayer habits, and help anchor the mind in focused prayer towards the Master.

Dominic reminds us to ensure that the posture of the heart, resembles the posture of the body, when bowing before the Cross of Jesus, bow before Him inwardly acknowledging Him as Lord overall, and Lord over you.

When being prostrate before the Lord, focus on the Feet of Jesus, focus on the very nature of the Savior, allow the mind, the heart and the body to become aligned to the Lord and hold your gaze upon the Cross-both in heart, and in mind. While the body is laid low, thus the gates of the heavenlies shall be opened to you, as you become a man with one mind; "not double-minded", receiving the blessing and mercy of Jesus upon your heart, you will feel the divine rest upon your heart.

QUESTIONS

1. What part of his life challenges you the most?

2. Which prayer movements do you like the most?

3. What impact does our body have on our spiritual development?

4. If we practice prayer, what changes the most in us?

5. Have you looked at your own prayer practice and thought some routines could change?

CHAPTER 7
Seraphim Sarov

"You cannot be too gentle, too kind. Shun even to appear harsh in your treatment of each other.

Joy, radiant joy, streams from the face of one who gives and kindles joy in the heart of one who receives." – Seraphim of Sarov

Born:	30 July 1754
Died:	15 January 1833 (73)
Nationality:	Russian
Location:	Sarvov – Russia
Outlook:	Eastern Orthodox
Biographer:	Seraphim Chichagov,
Books:	The Herald of God's Loving-Kindness
	Spiritual Exercises
Interests:	Theology
Achievements:	1000 nights of prayer
Key Teachings:	Contemplation, Self Denial
Supernatural Miracles:	Healing powers
	Gift of prophecy
Canonized:	19 July 1903

The Life of Saint Seraphim of Sarov

Seraphim (Prokhor Moshnin) was born on July 19, 1754, in Kursk Russia, to his parents Isidore and Agathia Moshnin, his father was a merchant trader.

In 1777 at the age of 19, he started as a novice at the monastery of Sarov, and in 1786 took his vows and was given the name Seraphim, meaning "fiery" or "burning one."

He was ordained as a monk in 1793 and became the leader of the Diveyevo Convent. Just after this, Seraphim moved into the woods and wilderness close to the monastery and lived the life of a hermit for 25 years.

After being attacked by robbers in the wilderness at one time, Seraphim spent 5 months in the Sarov Monastery, recovering from the wounds. This incident caused him to walk with a hunched back for the rest of his life.

In 1815 he allowed pilgrims into his hermitage for the first time for confession, this however changed as a steady stream of pilgrims became a flood of people searching for healing and his prophetic gifting.

He called his visitors "My Joy"; always affectionate in his greeting and loving to those who would seek his company.

Seraphim died on his knees before an Icon on 15th January 1833 (aged 73).

His relics were returned to Diveyevo Convent, after being held in Moscow, and on 19 October 2016, the Russain space program launched his relics into space aboard the Soyuz MS-02.

Theology of Saint Seraphim Sarov

"Whatever you do, do it gently and unhurriedly, because virtue is not a pear to be eaten in one bite."

Seraphim of Sarov

Life and Teaching of Saint Seraphim of Sarov – Page 415

If man does not care excessively for himself, because he is consumed by his love for God and by good deeds and he knows that God will take care of him, then such a hope is a true and wise hope. However if man counts on himself and his virtues only, and prays to God for help only when unforeseen troubles befall him and he cannot find means to avoid them and he hopes for God's help, then such a hope is false and in vain.

Life and Teaching of Saint Seraphim of Sarov – Page 430

He who loves himself cannot love God. And he who does not love himself because of his love for God, loves God truly. He who loves God truly considers himself a wanderer and a stranger on this earth, as he longs for God and his soul and mind are focused on contemplating Him only. A soul which is full of love for God will not fear the prince of the air even at the moment of its parting from the body. Considering the earth as a foreign land, such a soul will fly up, accompanied by Angels, to its homeland.

Life and Teaching of Saint Seraphim of Sarov – Page 435

He who is determined to follow the path of inner vigilance must first of all have the fear of God, which is the source of wisdom. Let the words of the prophet: 'Serve the Lord with fear, and rejoice with trembling.'(Ps.2, 11) be always imprinted on his mind. He must follow his path with utmost cautiousness and reverence in regard to all that is sacred, and not carelessly. Otherwise a terrifying sentence of God might be applied to him: 'Cursed be he that doeth the work of the Lord deceitfully,.' (Jer., 48, 10) Reverential cautiousness is required because the sea (that is man's heart with all its thoughts and desires, which should be purified by means of mindfulness) is enormous: 'So is this great and wide sea, wherein are things creeping innumerable,'

Life and Teaching of Saint Seraphim of Sarov – Page 446

However nobody is able to acquire the fear for God until he has freed himself from daily worries. When the mind becomes free from worries then it is driven by the fear of God and it aspires to Gods Grace.

Life and Teaching of Saint Seraphim of Sarov – Page 479

According to the teaching of the Holy Fathers every man is accompanied by two angels: one angel is the good one and another one is the evil one. The angel of good is quiet, meek and silent. When he enters man's heart he converses with the heart about truth, purity, honesty, serenity, good deeds and virtues. When you feel this in your heart then obviously this is the Angel of truth who visited you. The evil spirit is bitterly witty, cruel and mad. When he enters your heart you will recognize him through his deeds. (Anthony, Word 61)

Life and Teaching of Saint Seraphim of Sarov – Page 489

Make a mark in your mind and examine yourself regularly and incessantly and see which of your passions have become weaker, according to you? Which passions are exterminated and have left you in peace, which passions have started to subside because your soul is becoming healthier and not because of the fact that the causes of these passions are not there? Which passions have you learned to conquer by your reason, and not only by depriving yourself from the cause of these passions?

Life and Teaching of Saint Seraphim of Sarov – Page 493

Pay also heed to yourself, whether you can see that there is healthy flesh, that is, peace of soul, which grows in your decaying sore? Which passions attack you constantly and swiftly and what are the intervals between their attacks; are these bodily or spiritual passions or complex, mixed passions? Do they enter your memory as something weak or strong? Do they attack your soul like mighty ones or like sneaking thieves? How does your inner king, your mind, the

Life and Teaching of Saint Seraphim of Sarov – Page 497

Do they manifest themselves in vivid images or without them, just like a feeling; or, do they appear just in your memory, without causing a turbulence in you, thoughts about them and response in your soul? This is how you can measure the degree of your soul's health.

Life and Teaching of Saint Seraphim of Sarov – Page 565

through fire and through water: but thou broughtest us out into a wealthy place.' (Ps. 65, 12) The path of those who wish to please God is littered with many sorrows. How loudly should we praise the holy Martyrs for the suffering that they have undergone for God's sake, while we cannot even stand fever? Nothing is so favourable to acquire inner peace as one's silence and an incessant conversation with oneself and seldom conversation with others. And nothing is better than peace in Christ, as it destroys every attack of the aerial and earthly evil spirits. For 'our struggle is not against blood and flesh but against the sources and rulers of the darkness of this century, the spirits

Life and Teaching of Saint Seraphim of Sarov – Page 571

The sign of one's spiritual life is immersing in oneself and secret work inside one's heart. God's Grace dawns upon such a man and he comes into a peaceful frame of mind and through this he reaches the most peaceful state. A peaceful state comes from a clean conscience, but the most peaceful states comes when man contemplates with his mind the grace of the Holy Spirit inside himself, according to God's

Life and Teaching of Saint Seraphim of Sarov – Page 574

Can man not feel joy when he sees the sun with his physical eyes? But it is immeasurably more joyful when the mind sees by its inner eye the Sun of truth, Christ. Then man feels the joy that Angels feel. This is exactly what the Apostle called 'Our life is established in heaven' (Phil. 3, 20). He who firmly preserves a peaceful temper, extracts, as if with a spoon, spiritual gifts. The holy fathers lived long as they had a peaceful temper and were shielded by God's grace.

Life and Teaching of Saint Seraphim of Sarov – Page 579

When man acquires a peaceful temper, then he can pour out from himself the light of the illuminated mind also onto others. And until he has acquired such a state, he should keep in mind constantly the following words of Hannah the prophetess: 'let not proud words leave thy mouth' (1 Kings, 2,

Life and Teaching of Saint Seraphim of Sarov – Page 640

Then, first having purified the soul by repentance and good deeds, and with a sincere faith in the Crucified, one should close one's bodily eyes, immerse the mind in the heart and cry and call incessantly the name of our Lord Jesus Christ. Then, in proportion to the zeal and ardour of spirit towards the Beloved (Lk., 3, 22) man finds in the Name that he is invoking a delight, which will prompt him to search for the highest illumination. When the mind will stay long in the heart, doing this exercise, then the light of Christ will start to shine and will illuminate the chamber of the soul by Divine light, as God said through His prophet Malachi: 'But unto you that fear My name shall the Sun of righteousness arise' (Mal. 4, 2). This light is at the same time life, according to the words of the Gospel: 'In Him was life; and the life was the light of men.'

Life and Teaching of Saint Seraphim of Sarov – Page 647

When man contemplates inwardly the eternal light, then his mind is pure and does not have any material thoughts. It (the mind) becomes completely immersed in the contemplation of uncreated goodness and beauty, it forgets all which is matter and does not even want to see itself but it wishes to

Life and Teaching of Saint Seraphim of Sarov – Page 648

Hide in the core of the earth just in order not to be deprived of this, the true good: God.

Life and Teaching of Saint Seraphim of Sarov – Page 667

The fear of God awakens the sleeping conscience, and the conscience makes the soul see its ugliness as if in the mirror of a pure and unstirred water. This is how are born and grow still deeper the roots of repentance. We insult God's greatness during our entire life by our sins and therefore we should humbly ask the Lord to forgive us our debts. Is it possible for one who has received God's grace but has fallen, to rise up again through repentance? It is possible, according to the Psalmist: 'Thou hast thrust sore at me that I might fall: but the Lord helped me.

Life and Teaching of Saint Seraphim of Sarov – Page 711

The founder of the feat and our Saviour the Lord Jesus Christ, before He undertook the heroic deed of redemption of the human race, fortified Himself by a long period of fasting. And all the ascetics, when starting work for God, armed themselves by fasting and walked on the path of the cross during the feat of fasting only. They even considered the measure of their success in the ascetic practises by their success in fasting.

Life and Teaching of Saint Seraphim of Sarov – Page 731

We should not expose what is best kept inside our heart without necessity. Only then is what we have gathered secured against the visible and invisible enemies, when it is preserved like a treasure inside the heart. Do not open to all and everyone the secrets of your heart.

Life and Teaching of Saint Seraphim of Sarov – Page 736

But the most regretful of all is that it (verbosity) can extinguish that very fire that our Lord Jesus Christ came to cast into the ground of human hearts. Nothing cools so quickly the fire, which the Holy Spirit blows into the heart of the monk for the sanctification of his soul, as personal contacts with others and verbose conversations with them.

Life and Teaching of Saint Seraphim of Sarov - Page 890

Excessive care for worldly things is caused by lack of faith and faintheartedness. Woe unto us, if we, caring for ourselves, do not become firmly established in our hope in God, Who cares for us. If we do not ascribe to Him the visible good that we use in this temporary life, how can we expect from Him the good, which is promised to us in the future eternal life. Let us not be such sceptics, but let us better 'seek

Life and Teaching of Saint Seraphim of Sarov - Page 893

first the Kingdom of God, and all these things shall be added' (Math. 6, 33), according to the word of the Saviour. It is better for us to despise what is not ours, that is the temporary and corruptible; and to long for what is ours, the incorruptible and immortal. For when we will become incorruptible and immortal then we will be awarded the visible contemplation of God, like the Apostles, who saw the Divine Transfiguration. We will reach unity with God, which is beyond any comprehension, like the heavenly minds

Life and Teaching of Saint Seraphim of Sarov - Page 903

For the soul which is full of sadness becomes mad and frenzied and can neither accept a good advice quietly nor answer meekly to the questions put to it. Such a soul runs away from people, as if they are the cause of its confusion, because it does not understand that the cause of illness lies within itself. A sad monk does not prompt his mind to contemplate and he can never offer a pure prayer. The one who overcame his passions, at the same time overcame his sadness. However the one who is conquered by his passions will not be able to avoid the fetters of sadness. As an illness can be seen in the colour of the skin of the face, he who is possessed by passion is exposed by his sadness. He who loves the world, cannot be free from sadness. And he, who despises the world is always joyful.

Life and Teaching of Saint Seraphim of Sarov - Page 951

These are the reasons why Jesus Christ, the Son of God came into the world: 1. God's love for the human race: 'God loved the world so much that He gave His only-begotten Son' (Jn. 3, 16) 2. The restoration of the image and likeness of God in fallen man, as the holy Church sings (the 1st canon for the Nativity of Christ, the 1st song): 'Man who, being made in the image

Life and Teaching of Saint Seraphim of Sarov - Page 954

of God, had become corrupt through sin, and was full of vileness, and had fallen away from the better life Divine, doth the wise Creator restore anew.' 3. The salvation of human souls: 'For God sent not His Son into the world to condemn the world, but that the world through Him might be saved.'

Life and Teaching of Saint Seraphim of Sarov – Page 967

The active life serves the purpose of cleansing us from the sinful passions and elevates us to the perfection of acts. By this the active life paves the way for us for a contemplative life. For only those who cleansed themselves from passions and became perfect can lead a contemplative life, as it can be seen from the words of the Holy Scripture: 'blessed are the pure of heart as they shall see God' (Math. 5,8) and from the words of Gregory the Theologian: 'only the perfect can begin with contemplation safely.'

Dialogue Recorded with Motovilov

The miraculous transfiguration of the starets' face was described by a close admirer and follower of St. Seraphim: Motovilov. This happened during the winter, on a cloudy day. Motovilov was sitting on a stump in the woods; St. Seraphim was squatting across from him and telling his pupil the meaning of a Christian life, explaining for what we Christians live on earth.

"It is necessary that the Holy Spirit enter our heart. Everything good that we do, that we do for Christ, is given to us by the Holy Spirit, but prayer most of all, which is always available to us," he said.

"Father," answered Motovilov, "how can I see the grace of the Holy Spirit? How can I know if He is with me or not?"

St. Seraphim began to give him examples from the lives of the saints and apostles, but Motovilov still did not understand. The elder then firmly took him by the shoulder and said to him, "We are both now, my dear fellow, in the Holy Spirit." It was as if Motovilov's eyes had been opened, for he saw that the face of the elder was brighter than the sun. In his heart Motovilov felt joy and peace, in his body a warmth as if it were summer, and a fragrance began to spread around them. Motovilov was terrified by the unusual change, but especially by the fact that the face of the starets shone like the sun. But St. Seraphim said to him, "Do not fear, dear fellow. You would not even be able to see me if you yourself were not in the fullness of the Holy Spirit. Thank the Lord for His mercy toward us."

Thus Motovilov understood, in mind and heart, what the descent of the Holy Spirit and His transfiguration of a person meant.

My Experience with Saint Seraphim of Sarov

My first impression of Saint Seraphim was the power he carries and his ability to hide this power of God so as not to distract from the focus being Christ.

"Theosis"– the ability to transcend human nature and the human frame, becoming Christ-like, in a sense.

This is not a common teaching in Western Christianity, but a quite common teaching in the eastern orthodox church. Some would call it the "divinification" of man, however, this concept is controversial and hard to explain at best.

When the believer comes to Christ, we all know the believer is re-created into a new species, the bible clearly states the "new creation realities", however the complete implication of this then needs to be explored.

The final battle of humanity is the fear of death. There are those who have defeated this ancient foe, if we look at the biblical heroes; Enoch never died, Elijah never died; but transcended their death and were able to transfigure their bodies into a new dimension. Some would say the ever-living ones, those who took possession of the complete work of Jesus on the Cross, and then were able to defeat the normal law of sin and death.

The question becomes, which does Paul mean, when he says we have died with Christ, and now we are living with Him. This is not just a metaphor, but a true new creation reality; the baptism in water foreshadows the maturing of the believer, and shows the believer, awakened by Jesus, that the final fruition of the promise is complete resurrection ability, a concurring of death in a complete way.

Death for the new creation Christian, is not really an option, death cannot be part of the experience of this new species of creation, as the divine nature is imputed into the believer. Granted most have not attained this "enlightened" state, (I use this word specifically.) The light of Christ transforms, transfigures, and elevates the human frame beyond this current creation, and this current emanation of created existence.

I understood that when the bible says "kinos", it means completely created from ex-nelio; never before seen. God created a whole new being, a new dimension, a new creation, not just a new body for post-Christ Adam, Jesus went back into the beginning, and need to create a whole new place, a whole new realm, a completely new creation, which could be accessed by His nature and divine sacrifice in history.

This is the mystery hidden from the ages, that Jesus, because of the pre-foundation sacrifice, could access this place again, by dying on the cross,

Jesus could re-create creation.

This is only accessible after the cross; this was not accessible in the light record before the death of Jesus, his body gave access, not just to us, but to all the saints before. Jesus became the new timeline; I understood that David, and Isaiah, all those who prophesied in part and saw in the glass dimly, saw Jesus, but never partook of this mystery, before the moment of death. Jesus re-created the whole creation, to enable this change, since we have become the new "adamic" race, and everything in creation existed inside Adam, when Jesus died for us, and the spirit was poured out on us, this "kinos-being" needed to be re-created as the summary of the new creation to come.

When John says, "I see a new Jerusalem above", he sees a completely new creation. When the bible talks about "tasting of the powers of the age to come", this age still needs to be entered into, when Jesus comes again and becomes the ruler on the throne, the powers of the age to come, will then become the powers of His divine age. The age of "homo sapiens" comes to an end, and the age of "homo-kinos" comes into the timeline of history. The true sons take their "estate" – their inheritance becomes Christ, and they start reflecting the divinity of Jesus to the whole cosmos.

Seraphim was eager to stress the doctrine of Theosis was not an equality with God, nor the complete elimination of the nature of humanity, what would then be the point of creating Adam in the first place.

The Theosis of the believer is always in part; this part might be bigger than most believers deem acceptable, since God is less worried about sharing His divinity than most believers. Since God can never be "Not God", His divine insecurity about His nature does not exist. Our lack of understanding of the divine nature brings us to a place of insecurity, where we feel the need to fight and defend the true size of our God box.

Jesus transfigured the body, to create a record of incarnation, He expects us to co-habit our new creation bodies with Him and become true temples of God. If Jesus says, "My house will be a house of prayer for all nations", He means you!!

How will you contain all nations inside of you? In the darkness of Genesis God created creation, the multi-verse, and in the Darkness that followed the death of Jesus, God once again created with Jesus a new moment, a new future, a new race of beings, that would co-exist with God in one Body, a place of worship, prayer and constant divinity.

The non-locality of matter that has been discovered by quantum science helps us make peace with this fact, however, the implications are staggering.

The worldwide temple web of believers has become a cloud network of interconnected believers, that span space, time, and reality. Interconnected by our co-inclusion in Christ, our global reality, this tent of David has been revived in our day, does the bible not call the body a tent? David might not need another tent meeting, or a tent revival, he might have a global tent already, called the church of Jesus Christ.

Economic systems that bring separation, wealth systems that want to trade with the body of Jesus will be something that needs to change in the future. Jesus is throwing the tables over again, and this time, He will not allow another system to govern His divine body. Prayer is an outflow of intimacy, trading on this like they did in the day of Jesus will no longer be acceptable. Revelation and information trading will change in the future. The knowledge economy based on the tree of knowledge will disappear, and become an experience economy, based on relationships, experiences, and moments of treasure. Heaven values what the earth discards, relationships are already the currency of social media, now it will become the only currency of the future.

We do not need a kingdom culture, if God wanted all the nations to be the same, the tribes of the earth and the nations of the world would not appear before His throne. God wants the diversity of nature reflected in the diversity of the culture of heaven. Heaven exists because identity has been secured, everybody knows Abba loves them, hence their unity and union with Jesus creates the foundation for diversity and unique expressions.

QUESTIONS

1. What church was Seraphim Sarov part of when he started?

2. Considering he wrote about the Holy Spirit, do you think he understood the Holy Spirit?

3. Which parts of his spiritual practice inspired you the most?

4. What is the difference between "Theosis" and "Divinification"?

5. When considering the effect that Seraphim Sarov had on the Russian church, could we imitate him to change our own systems and structures?

CHAPTER 8
Saint Bernard of Clairvaux

"There are those who seek knowledge for the sake of knowledge; that is Curiosity.

There are those who seek knowledge to be known by others; that is Vanity.

There are those who seek knowledge in order to serve; that is Love."

- Bernard of Clairvaux

CHAPTER 8 – Saint Bernard of Clairvaux

Born:	1090
Died:	20 August 1153
Nationality:	France
Location:	Clairvaux (France)
Outlook:	Catholic (Cistercians)
Books:	De gradibus humilitatis et superbiae [The steps of humility and pride] (in Latin). c. 1120
	De diligendo Dei [On loving God] (in Latin). Outlines seven stages of ascent leading to union with God
	Sermons on the Song of Songs (86)
	De gratia et libero arbitrio [On grace and free choice] (in Latin). c1128
Interests:	Theologian, Mystic, writer, Poet
Achievements:	Doctor of the church, Abbot of a Community
Key Teachings:	Lectio Divina (Contemplation)
Canonized:	18 January 1174

The Life of Saint Bernard of Clairvaux

Bernard was born in 1090, on the outskirts of Dijon in Burgundy to a noble family. His father Tescelin de Fontaine was the Lord of "Fontaine-lès-Dijon", and his mother was Alèthe de Montbard. Both his parents were part of the French noble class of that time in Burgundy.

Bernard was the third son of six boys, and he also had a sister. By the age of nine years, Bernard was sent to school at Châtillon-sur-Seine. Bernard loved language and words! He studied literature and poems, and it is believed that his focus on words was due to his passion for biblical studies.

He studied the Bible diligently and thus changed the face of Christianity to focus on a more personal faith as he experienced God in this manner as he was engaging in the bible. With Christ being the example, and the Virgin Mary being the intersensory bridge, between man and God.

He is often quoted; saying Mary Magdalene was the "chief of the apostles."

At the age of 19, his mother died, and Bernard sought to become a priest in the Cistercian order. When Bernard turned 22, while in prayer, he felt called to enter the Alberic of Cîteaux, to become a monk in the order. So, in 1113, Bernard and 30 of his followers were admitted into the monastic life by Stephen Harding, the Abbot of Cîteaux.

Due to the rapid expansion of the community, Bernard was sent out with 12 monks to Vallée d'Absinthe, in the Diocese of Langres. Bernard named the monastery Claire Vallée. He was ordained as the abbot of the third Cistercian monastery, at Clairvaux by William of Champeaux, Bishop of Châlons-sur-Marne.

In 1118, Clairvaux was able to find its first house – the first of some 70 Cistercian monasteries Bernard founded, and then exploded by his brothers, to 100 more monasteries during Bernard's lifetime.

Bernard had a strong diplomatic temperament, and he was able to build relationships with other orders like the Carthusians and the Premonstratensians. He also wrote the Rule for the new order during his time, the Knights Templar, in some sense the military wing of the church, who swore to defend the Holy Land "Israel", against the Turks.

Bernard would preside as secretary over the Council of Troyes, convoked by Pope Honorius II. He was pivotal in some of the dogmatic disputes between the bishops. On 14 February 1130, the well-known Schism erupted in Rome, when two people were elected for the role of the Pope: Pope Innocent II and Antipope Anacletus II.

This situation created chaos in the church, with some Royalty and Clergy in the same country being on different sides of the argument. Bernard was an expert negotiator, arbitrating affairs between opposing sides, he supported Pope Innocent II, and went to England and Germany to resolve the situation. Anacletus died on 25 January 1138, ending the stalemate of the situation, and resulting in the church once again being able to unify other one authority.

One of Bernard's students, Pope Eugene III, was elected in 1145, this gave Bernard unique influence in Rome.

As an acclaimed theologian, Bernard was trusted to deal with the heresies besetting the church at the time. He dealt with the Petrobrusians and the Henricians, by going to the south of France and preaching against their theology. He also preached against Catharism, a Gnostic sect, which believed, in two gods: one Good and one Evil. The god of the Old Testament was Evil, and the god of the New Testament was Good. This did not agree with the monotheism held by most of Christianity.

Louis VII of France asked Bernard to help with the recruitment of soldiers for the Second Crusade. Bernard preached one of the best sermons in his life to enroll the crowd, this sermon and his continued support in France aided the recruitment for the second crusade. The second crusade, however, was a complete failure, and most of the failure was blamed on Bernard, as the figurehead of the campaign.

Bernard died on 20 August 1153, at the age of 63. His grave was at Clairvaux Abbey, which was later moved to Troyes Cathedral.

Visions of Saint Bernard of Clairvaux

Loving God – Page 7

The earth under the ancient curse brought forth thorns and thistles; but now the Church beholds it laughing with flowers and restored by the grace of a new benediction. Mindful of the verse, 'My heart danceth for joy, and in my song will I praise Him', she re- freshes herself with the fruits of His Passion which she gathers from the Tree of the Cross, and with the flowers of His

Resurrection whose fragrance invites the frequent visits of her Spouse.

Loving God – Page 8

'One generation shall praise Thy works unto another and declare Thy power' (Ps. 145.4). Among us on the earth there is His memory; but in the Kingdom of heaven His very Presence. That Presence is the joy of those who have already attained to beatitude; the memory is the comfort of us who are still wayfarers, journeying towards the Fatherland.

Loving God – Page 10

Rightly then may she exult, 'His left hand is under my head and His right hand doth embrace me.' The left hand signifies the memory of that matchless love, which moved Him to lay down His life for His friends; and the right hand is the Beatific Vision which He hath promised to His own, and the delight they have in His presence. The Psalmist sings raptur- ously, 'At Thy right hand there is pleasure for evermore' (Ps. 16.11): so we are warranted in explaining the right hand as that divine and deifying joy of His presence.

Loving God – Page 10

What could result from the contemplation of compassion so marvelous and so undeserved, favor so free and so well attested, kindness so unexpected, clemency so unconquerable, grace so amazing except that the soul should withdraw from all sinful affections, reject all that is inconsistent with God's love, and yield herself wholly to heavenly things? No wonder is it that the Bride, moved by the perfume of these unctions, runs swiftly, all on fire with love, yet reckons herself as loving all too little in return for the Bridegroom's love. And rightly, since it is no great matter that a little dust should be all consumed with love of that Majesty which loved her first and which revealed itself as wholly bent on saving her. For 'God so loved the world that He gave His only-begotten Son, that whosoever believeth in Him should not perish but have everlasting life' (John 3.16).

Loving God – Page 15

On a lower plane of action, it is the reluctant, not the eager, whom we urge by promises of reward. Who would think of paying a man to do what he was yearning to do already? For instance no one would hire a hungry man to eat, or a thirsty man to drink, or a mother to nurse her own child. Who would think of bribing a farmer to dress his own vineyard, or to dig about his orchard, or to rebuild his house? So, all the more, one who loves God truly asks no other recompense than God Himself; for if he should demand anything else it would be the prize that he loved and not God.

Loving God – Page 22

"O chaste and holy love! O sweet and gracious affection! O pure and cleansed purpose, thoroughly washed and purged from any admixture of selfishness, and sweetened by contact with the divine will! To reach this state is to become godlike. As a drop of water poured into wine loses itself, and takes the color and savor of wine; or as a bar of iron, heated red-hot, becomes like fire itself, forgetting its own nature; or as the air, radiant with sun-beams, seems not so much to be illuminated as to be light itself; so in the saints all human affections melt away by some unspeakable transmutation into the will of God. For how could God be all in all, if anything merely human remained in man? The substance will endure, but in another beauty, a higher power, a greater glory. When will that be? Who will see, who possess it? '

Loving God – Page 25

I have drunk My wine with My milk' (Cant. 5.1). For the soul mixes with the wine of God's love the milk of natural affection, that is, the desire for her body and its glorification. She glows with the wine of holy love which she has drunk; but she is not yet all on fire, for she has tempered the potency of that wine with milk. The unmingled wine would enrapture the soul and make her wholly unconscious of self; but here is no such transport for she is still desirous of her body. When that desire is appeased, when the one lack is supplied, what should hinder her then from yielding herself utterly to God, losing her own likeness and being made like unto Him? At last she attains to that chalice of the heavenly wisdom, of which it is written, 'My cup shall be full.' Now indeed she is refreshed with the abundance of the house of God, where all selfish, carking care is done away, and where, for ever safe, she drinks the fruit of the vine, new and pure, with Christ in the Kingdom of His Father (Matt. 26.29).

Loving God – Page 27

So long as Thou doest well unto him, he will speak good of Thee' (Ps. 49.18, Vulg.). One praises God because He is mighty, another because He is gracious, yet another solely because He is essential goodness. The first is a slave and fears for himself; the second is greedy, desiring further benefits; but the third is a son who honors his Father. He who fears, he who profits, are both concerned about self-interest. Only in the son is that charity which seeketh not her own (I Cor. 13.5). Wherefore I take this saying, 'The law of the Lord is an undefiled law, converting the soul' (Ps. 19.7) to be of charity; because charity alone is able to turn the soul away from love of self and of the world to pure love of God

Song of Songs – Sermon 74, Experiences with the "Word"

Now bear with my foolishness a little. I want to tell you of my own experience, as I promised. Not that it is of any importance .... I admit that the Word has also come to me-I speak as a fool-and has come many times—But although he has come to me, I have never been conscious of the moment of his coming. I perceived his presence, I remembered afterwards that he had been with me; some times I had a presentiment that he would come, but I was never conscious of his coming or his going. And where he comes from when he visits my soul, and where he goes, and by what means he enters and goes out, I admit that I do not know even now; as John says: 'You do not know where he comes from or where he goes.' There is nothing strange in this, for of him was it said, 'Your foot steps will not be known.' The coming of the Word was not perceptible to my eyes, for he has not color; nor to the ears, for there was no sound; nor yet to my nostrils, for he mingles with the mind, not the air; he has not acted upon the air, but created it. His coming was not tasted by the mouth, for there was not eating or drinking, nor could he be known by the sense of touch, for he is not tangible. How then did he enter? Perhaps he did not enter because he does not come from outside? He is not one of the things which exist outside us. Yet he does not come from within me, for he is good, and I know there is no good in me. I have ascended to the highest in me, and look! the word is towering above that. In my curiosity I have descended to explore my lowest depths, yet I found him even deeper. If I look outside myself, I saw him stretching beyond the furthest I could see; and if I looked within, he was yet further within. Then I knew the truth of what I had read, 'In him we live and move and have our being'. And blessed is the man in whom he has his being, who lives for him and is moved by him.

My Journey with Saint Bernard of Clairvaux

Encountering Bernard, it became noticeably clear that he was careful with the discipline of his life. Every time he would pray, he made sure he was keeping the rule, and praying according to the right times of day, the right prayers, and the right moments.

Then something happened to him: as he spent hours reading the scriptures, he started seeing how time was not measured the same in heaven, and his moments with God, doing the disciplines of the faith became easier as the "tick-box" manner of the rule, changed into a relationship.

He started showing me his view of the church of Jesus Christ on the earth today and explained the tapestry of eternity. The Face of Jesus was being woven by the frequencies of the believers, and like a very complicated Persian carpet, the image was being made clearer.

God is not energy, although He manifests Himself through energy, nor is He frequency, but manifests Himself through energy. God is completely above and beyond what any human mind can understand. God is inside of creation manifesting Himself to us, while we are inside of creation, however, God also manifests Himself in heaven.

God stands outside of time and space, and even all of creation, even spiritual dimensions, God exists completely on His own, hence He was able to create in the first place. At once, God stands with one "foot" in conceptual reality and with the other "foot" outside everything we currently know about, or ever will know about, even while in heaven.

I saw every child of God, like a stand of color, frequencies and all kinds of patterns, being woven together, into this image of the face of Jesus, However the face was ever-changing, as humanity changed and interacted with God. This is one of the reasons, the church has not agreed on the face of Jesus, and why Abba has not allowed the world to create a face for His Son.

God created Adam, "Man", to be the image, and in the New Testament, created Christians to bear His divine likeness. We are supposed to reflect and become the divine tapestry reflected to all creation, and every dimension, and every realm. One could say, the divine paintbrush of God is filled with colors that are unlimited, frequency that is unending, and patterns that are ever-changing, on the canvas of spaceless creation, where there are no limits of time.

In this place, only the Holy Spirit can empower the believer to comprehend, since our own ability to understand, process and comprehend is so limited, the Holy Spirit literally comes to expand our bandwidth and builds divine structures of understanding into our grid of reality. To help us come to a place of knowing, not in a complete way, but at least knowing to enable a relationship with the divine.

The ultimate goal for any process in the spiritual reality is to build a relationship; Abba wants His kids to grow in maturity, and in understanding of His divine reality. A Father will never achieve a mature relationship with His children, if they cannot comprehend the basic milieu of their Dad.

All spiritual discipline, all meditation, contemplation, and prayer, is focused on the efforts of man to become sensitized, enlightened, and more adept at apprehending the spiritual nuance of God's movement on the material plane of existence.

God's "father heart" is always to surround you, to encompass every part of who you are, with His presence, and then to slowly wait for you to discover the very slight movements of His love, in your world, where you have only allowed Him a very little space to move. Slowly as you mature, your ability to feel the light breeze of His breath, allows you to know, God is in the room, He lives in you, and He lives with you.

QUESTIONS

1. Which part of his life story inspired you the most?

2. From the extracts of his writings which part did you enjoy the most?

3. Do you think our understanding of God's love is changing?

4. If humanity and technology is increasing, do you think our understanding of spiritual realities can also change?

CHAPTER 9
John of Ruysbroeck

"If above all things we would taste God, and feel eternal life in ourselves, we must go forth into God with our feeling, above reason; and there we must abide, onefold, empty of ourselves, and free from images, lifted up by love into the simple bareness of our intelligence." – John Ruysbroeck

CHAPTER 9 - John of Ruysbroeck

Born:	1293
Died:	2 December 1381 (87)
Nationality:	Flemish (Dutch)
Location:	Ruisbroek	Brussels
Outlook:	Catholic
Books:	The Sparkling Stone
	The Spiritual Espousals
Interests:	Mystical Theology
Achievements:	Spontaneously combusted in the forest (Divine Seraphic Nature)
Key Teachings:	Passion of Jesus Christ, Detachment

The Life of John of Ruysbroeck

"Knowledge of ourselves teaches us whence we come, where we are and whither we are going. We come from God and we are in exile; and it is because our potency of affection lends towards God that we are aware of this state of exile."

John of Ruysbroeck

John was born in 1293 in Ruisbroek, in the little village of Ruusbroec. We know that his mother was a devoted catholic, but little is known about his father. The village is situated between Brussels and Hal.

At the age of 11, John ran away from home to his uncle John Hinckaert, at the Cathedral of St Gudule in Brussels. His uncle at the age of 40 renounced all his worldly possessions and stayed with a friend, Francis van Coudenberg, they both lived a very simple life and welcomed the young man into their home, where self-denial, and humility were their only possessions.

Although they did not have much, his uncle paid for his education, with the intention of John to become a priest. John was indeed ordained as a priest in 1318, at Saint Gudule's church. His mother died shortly before his ordination. She had followed him to Brussels and joined a Beguine community while she was still alive.

John was a priest from 1318 to 1343 at St Gudula. He still stayed with his uncle and their friend in extremely austere circumstances, committing to the vow of poverty and asceticism.

During his time as a priest a lady called Bloemardinne, who preached quietism, and pantheism, was gaining great popularity with her teachings. John wrote many pamphlets, and other theological works to combat the clear heresy she was proclaiming to the community in Brussels.

John served the community until he was 50 years old, and then decided the time for a more retired and secluded life had come. In 1343, John, his uncle and friend moved to a hermitage in Groenedaal, they also attended to the monastery in the forest of Soignes, which was given to them by the Duke of Barabant, John, the 3rd.

Due to the growth in their followers streaming to their hermitage, they created the Priory of Groenendael, according to the Rule of Augustine. Coutenberg thus became the Provost.

Most of John's writings and mystical works seem to emanate from the silence he was able to have in the woods, although already known in Brussels as an "illuminated man", his true genius was only to blossom in nature, and quite a silence.

He would often write mystical works while sitting under a specific tree, as the Spirit would come upon him, he would withdraw there, to write, as the Holy Spirit would guide him, in this sacred place of ecstasy.

In his old age, with greater trouble to see clearly, he would ask a younger brother to accompany him and dictate his words to the waiting scribe. As a skilled director of spiritual growth, many traveled to hear his wisdom. He had good relationships with other orders of the church like the Carthusian house at Herne, and the community of Poor Clare Franciscans situated in the area.

In 1378, he was visited by Geert Groote, whom he told about his writing and with "Great gentleness and humility," he explained the divine inspiration of his writing.

John had many ecstasies and spiritual experiences with Jesus Christ appearing to him, the Saints, and the blessed Virgin, while he was saying mass, or in passionate devotion to the Eucharist.

On one occasion, having slowly slipped ways from his social commitments, he was sitting under his favorite tree, rapt in ecstasy, encapsulated by an aura of the radiant presence of light.

John was a man who loved his friends, and those who would seek his council, every person that left him testified of great insight, wisdom, and divine love flowing from his words.

John Ruysbroeck died on 2 December 1381, at the age of 82, in Groenendaal.

The Theology of John of Ruysbroeck

"When love has carried us above all things into the Divine Dark, there we are transformed by the Eternal Word Who is the image of the Father; and as the air is penetrated by the sun, thus we receive in peace the Incomprehensible Light, enfolding us, and penetrating us."

John of Ruysbroeck

One needs to understand that Ruysbroeck discussed some major topics of revelation for his era. One of his chief theological endeavors was to discuss the theology of the trinity, something we in the West seem to shy away from, since this topic is so hard to comprehend with mere rationalism. John was able to draw from some of the Eastern church theology, and start discussing the "divinification" of man, or as some would say "theosis" of man.

The complex descriptions of this process, in the paradoxical explanations of God as both Three and also God is One, makes the theological task a very difficult task, and even harder to explain. At some point human language fails the most eloquent theologians and philosophers, in our task to explain the divine, we will all on some level fail.

Our best effort is to invent some language, re-define some concepts, and contribute to the human journey of experience and define God's existence and the nuance of His ways.

God is God, and we are men, and being men, have limitations, yet being compassionate in nature, God allows us to define Him to others, with our dripping ink, we scratch our words, and hope to some, they might find some light in them.

Book 2 – Chapter 1, Page 1: How to see in the Spiritual Dimensions

The first is the light of Divine grace, and this in a more lofty degree than that which we can experience in the outward and active life without earnest inward diligence. The second thing is the casting out of all distracting images and attachments from the heart; so that the man may be free and imageless, released from all attachments, and empty of all creatures. The third thing is a free turning of the will, with a gathering together of all our powers, both bodily and ghostly, cleansed from every inordinate love. Thereby the will flows forth into the unity of God and into the unity of the mind; and thus the rational creature may obtain and possess the most high unity of God in a supernatural manner.

Book 2 – Page 3: Levels of Unity

The first and highest unity of man is in God; for all creatures depend upon this unity for their being, their life, and their preservation; and if they be separated in this wise from God, they fall into the nothingness and become nought. This unity is in us essentially, by nature, whether we be good or evil. And without our own working it makes us neither holy nor blessed. This unity we possess within us and yet above us, as the ground and the preserver of our being and of our life.

Book 2 - Page 45: The Communing of Christ to the Believer

Christ, the glorious Sun, the Divine Brightness, by His inward coming and by the power of His Spirit, enlightens and brightens and enkindles the free heart and all the powers of the soul. And this is the first work of the inward coming in the exercise of desire. Like as the power and the nature of fire enkindles everything which is offered to the flames, so Christ, by the fiery ardour of His inward coming, enkindles every ready, free and uplifted heart; and in this coming He says: Go ye out by exercises according to the way of this coming.

Book 2 - Page 46: Devotion to God

Of this sensible love is born devotion to God and to His glory. For none can have within his heart the hunger of devotion save him who bears within himself a sensible love of God. Where the fire of love sends up the flames of its desire to heaven, there is devotion. Devotion moves and draws a man, both from without and from within, towards the service of God. Devotion makes body and soul to blossom in nobility and worth before God and before all men. Devotion is demanded of us by God in every service which we ought to do to Him. Devotion purifies the body and the soul of everything that can stop and hinder us. Devotion shows and bestows the right way at blessedness.

Book 2 - Page 49: Spiritual Inebriation

From this rapturous delight springs spiritual inebriation. Spiritual inebriation is this; that a man receives more sensible joy and sweetness than his heart can either contain or desire. Spiritual inebriation brings forth many strange gestures in men. It makes some sing and praise God because of their fulness of joy, and some weep with great tears because of their sweetness of heart. It makes one restless in all his limbs, so that he must run and jump and dance; and so excites another that he must gesticulate and clap his hands. Another cries out with a loud voice, and so shows forth the plenitude he feels within; another must be silent and melt away, because of the rapture which he feels in all his senses. At times he thinks that all the world must feel what he feels: at times he thinks that none can taste what he has attained.

Book 2 - Page 52: Restless longing for God

In the like season of the year, the visible sun enters the sign of Leo, that is, the Lion, who is fierce by nature, for he is the lord over all beasts. So likewise, when a man comes to this way, Christ, the bright Sun, stands in the sign of the Lion, for the rays of His heat are so fierce that the blood in the heart of the impatient man must boil. And when this fierce way prevails, it masters and subdues all other ways and works; for it wills to be wayless, that is, without manner. And in this tumult a man sometimes falls into a desire and restless longing to be freed from the prison of his body, so that he may at once be united with Him Whom he loves. And he opens his inward eyes and beholds the heavenly house full of glory and joy, and his Beloved crowned in the midst of it, flowing forth towards His saints in abounding bliss; whilst he must lack all this. And therefrom there often spring in such a man outward tears and great longings. He looks down and considers the place of exile in which he has been imprisoned, and from which he cannot escape; then tears of sadness and misery gush forth.

Book 2 – Page 52: Ecstasies and Divine Revelations

Sometimes a man may also be drawn above himself and above the spirit (but not altogether outside himself) into an Incomprehensible Good, which he shall never be able either to utter or to explain in the way in which he heard and saw; for in this simple act and this simple vision, to hear and to see are one. And none can work this in man, without intermediary and without the co-operation of any creature, save God alone. It is called Raptus; which means, rapt away, or uplifted, or carried away. At times God grants to such men a sudden spiritual glimpse, like the lightning in the sky. It comes like a sudden glimpse of strange brightness, shining forth from the Simple Nudity. And thereby for an instant the spirit is raised above itself; but the light passes at once and the man returns to himself again. This is the work of God Himself; it is something very sublime; for those to whom it happens often become illuminated men.

Book 2 – Page 56: The fourth degree of the coming of Christ in the believer

When the sun first begins to descend from the zenith to the nadir, it enters the sign which is called Virgo, that is, the Virgin, because now the season becomes unfruitful, as a virgin is. (In this time the glorious Virgin Mary, the mother of Christ,

ascended to heaven full of joy and rich in all virtues.) At this time the heat begins to grow less; and men begin to gather in, for use during the rest of the year, those ripe and lasting fruits which can be kept and consumed long afterwards, such as corn and wine and the durable fruits, which have now come to their maturity. And a part of the same corn is sown, so that it be multiplied for the benefit of men. In this season all the work of the sun of the whole year is perfected and fulfilled.

So likewise, when Christ the glorious Sun has risen to the zenith in a man's heart, as I have taught you in the third degree; and when He then begins to *descend and to hide the shining of His Divine rays and to forsake the man; then the heat and impatience of love begin to grow less. Now when Christ thus hides Himself, and withdraws the shining of His brightness and His heat, this is the first work, and the new coming, of this degree. Then Christ speaks in ghostly wise within this man, saying: "Go ye out in such wise as I will now show you." So the man goes out, and finds himself poor and miserable and forsaken.*

Book 2 – Page 63: Rungs in the ladder of God

The first rill of grace, which God causes to flow forth in this coming, is a pure simplicity, shining in the spirit without differentiation. This rill takes its rise from the fountain within the unity of the spirit; and it flows straight downwards and pours through all the powers of the soul, the lower and the higher; and raises them above all multiplicity and all busyness and produces simplicity in a man; and shows and gives him the inward bond of unity of spirit. Thus he is lifted up as regards his memory, and is freed from distracting images and from fickleness.

Book 2 – Page 66: Going towards God

This rich and enlightened man shall distribute gifts to all the angelic choirs, and all spirits, each in particular according to its merits, out of the richness of his God and out of the generosity of his own ground; which is illuminated and overflowing with great and wonderful gifts. He passes through all choirs, through all hierarchies and orders, and beholds how God dwells in all according to the merit of each. This enlightened man goes swiftly and in ghostly wise round and through all the heavenly hosts, rich and overflowing with charity, and enriching and inundating the whole celestial company with fresh glory out of the Richness and Abundance of the Trinity and Unity of the Divine Nature.

Book 2 – Page 84: The Spirit of Understanding

And therefore God gives him the sixth gift, which is the spirit of Understanding. This gift we have already likened to a fountain with three rills, for it establishes our spirit in the unity, it reveals Truth and it brings forth a wide and general love. This gift may also be likened to sunshine, for by its shining the sun fills the air with a simple brightness and lights all forms, and shows the distinctions of all colours. And thereby it shows forth its own power; and its heat is common to the whole world, bringing forth fruits and useful things. So likewise does the first ray of this gift bring about simplicity within the spirit. And this simplicity is penetrated by a particular radiance even as the air of the heavens by the splendour of the sun. For the grace of God, which is the ground of all gifts, maintains itself essentially like to a simple light in our potential understanding: and, by means of this simple light our spirit is made stable and onefold and enlightened, and fulfilled of grace and Divine gifts: and here it is like unto God through grace and Divine love.

Book 2 – Page 94: Passive Grace that Perverts the Soul

Now we find yet another kind of perverted men, who are in some points different from those already described; though they too believe themselves to be exempted from all works, and to be instruments with which God works what He wills. And therefore they say that they are in a purely passive state without activity; and that the works which God works through them are noble and meritorious beyond anything that another man, working his works himself by the grace of God, could do. And therefore they say that they are God-passive men, and that they do nothing of themselves, but that God works all their works. And they say they can do no sin: for it is God Who does all their works, and in themselves they are empty of all things. And all that God wills is worked through them, and nothing else. These men have surrendered themselves to inward passivity in

their emptiness; and live without preference for any one thing. And they have a resigned and humble appearance, and can very well endure and suffer with equanimity all that befalls them; for they hold themselves to be the instruments with which God works according to His will. Such men in many of their ways and works are like in their conduct to good men, but in some things they differ from them; for all things to which they are inwardly urged, whether these be virtuous or not, they believe to proceed from the Holy Ghost. And in this and in suchlike things, they are deceived;

The Sparkling Stone – Page 103: Union with God

Through this inward exercise, he reaches the third state; which is that he feels a ghostly union with God. Whosoever then has, in his inward exercise, an imageless and free ascent unto his God, and means nought else but the glory of God, must taste of the goodness of God; and he must feel from within a true union with God. And in this union, the inward and spiritual life is made perfect; for in this union, the desirous power is perpetually enticed anew and stirred to new inward activity. And by each act, the spirit rises upwards to a new union. And so activity and union perpetually renew themselves; and this perpetual renewal in activity and in union is a ghostly life. And so you are now able to see how a man becomes good through the moral virtues and an upright intention; and how he may become ghostly through the inward virtues and union with God.

The Sparkling Stone – Page 105: Jesus as the Stone

I give to eat of the hidden manna, that is, an inward and hidden savour and celestial joy; and will give him a sparkling stone, and in the stone a new name written which no man knoweth saving he that receiveth it. This stone is called a pebble, for it is so small that it does not hurt when one treads on it. This stone is shining white and red like a flame of fire; and it is small and round, and smooth all over, and very light. By this sparkling stone we mean our Lord Christ Jesus, for He is, according to His Godhead, a shining forth of the Eternal Light, and an irradiation of the glory of God, and a flawless mirror in which all things live. Now to him who overcomes and transcends all things, this sparkling stone is given; and with it he receives light and truth and life.

The Sparkling Stone – Page 110: The difference between Hidden sons, and Secret Friends of God

And so there is a great difference between the secret friends and the hidden sons of God. For the friends feel nought else but a loving and living ascent to God in some wise, but, above this, the sons experience a simple and death-like passing which is in no wise.

The inward life of the friends of our Lord is an upward-striving exercise of love, wherein they desire to remain for ever with their own selfhood; but how one possesses God through bare love above every exercise, in freedom from one's self, this they do not feel.

The Sparkling Stone – Page 112: How to achieve Sonship

But if above all things we would taste God, and feel eternal life in ourselves, we must go forth into God with our feeling, above reason; and there we must abide, onefold, empty of ourselves, and free from images, lifted up by love into the simple bareness of our intelligence. For when we go out in love beyond and above all things, and die to all observation in ignorance and in darkness, then we are wrought and transformed through the Eternal Word, Who is the Image of the Father. In this idleness of our spirit, we receive the Incomprehensible Light, which enwraps us and penetrates us, as the air is penetrated by the light of the sun. And this Light is nothing else than a fathomless staring and seeing

The Sparkling Stone – Page 114: The Love Immersion

This immersion is essential, and is closely bound up with the state of love: and so it continues whether we sleep or whether we wake, whether we know it or whether we know it not. And so it does not earn for us any new degree of reward; but it maintains us in the possession of God and of all that good which we have received. And this down-sinking is like a river, which without pause or turning back ever pours into the sea; since this is its proper resting-place. So likewise when we possess God alone, the down-sinking of our being, with the love that belongs to it flows forth, without return, into a fathomless experience which we possess, and which is our proper resting-place. Were we always simple, and could we always contemplate with the same recollection, we should always have the same experience.

The Sparkling Stone – Page 118: The Mountain of Transfiguration

And so, that the Name of Christ may be exalted and glorified in us, we should follow Him up the mountain of our bare intelligence, even as Peter, James and John followed Him on to mount Thabor. Thabor means in our tongue an increase of light. So soon as we are like Peter in knowledge of truth, and like James in the overcoming of the world, and like John in fulness of grace possessing the virtues in righteousness; then Jesus brings us up on to the mountain of our bare intelligence to a hidden solitude, and reveals Himself to us in glory and in Divine brightness. And, in His name, His Father in heaven opens to us the living book of His Eternal Wisdom. And the Wisdom of God enfolds our bare vision and the simplicity of our spirit in a wayless, simple fruition of all good without distinction; and here there are indeed seeing and knowing, tasting and feeling, essence and life, having and being: and all this is one in our transcendence in God.

The Book of Supreme Truth – 127: Why some don't attain Mediated Union with God

But now you may ask me why all good men do not attain to feel this. Now listen and I will tell you the why and the wherefore. They do not respond to the stirring of God with a forsaking of themselves, and so they do not abide with quickening fervour before the Presence of God; and also they are not careful of heart in their inward self-examination. And therefore they always remain more outward and manifold than inward and simple, and they work their works more from good custom than from inward feeling. And they care more for particular methods and the greatness and multiplicity of good works than for the intention and love towards God. And so they remain outward and manifold of heart, and are not aware of how God lives in them with the fulness of grace.

The Book of Supreme Truth – 127: Distinction between God and Man in union

Yet the creature does not become God, for the union takes place in God through grace and our homeward-turning love: and therefore the creature in its inward contemplation feels a distinction and an otherness between itself and God. And though the union is without means, yet the manifold works which God works in heaven and on earth are nevertheless hidden from the spirit. For though God gives Himself as He is, with clear discernment, He gives Himself in the essence of the soul, where the powers of the soul are simplified above reason, and where, in simplicity, they suffer the transformation of God. There all is full and overflowing, for the spirit feels itself to be one truth and one richness and one unity with God. Yet even here there is an essential tending forward, and therein is an essential distinction between the being of the soul and the Being of God

The Book of Supreme Truth – 132: Jesus prays for Union

Further, Christ prayed thus, that He might be in us and we in Him. This we find in the Gospel, in many places. And this is the union without means; for the Love of God is not only outpouring, but it also draws us inwards, into the Unity. And those who feel and are aware of this, become inward and enlightened men, and their highest powers are uplifted, above all exercises, into their naked being: and there, above reason, the powers become simplified in their essence, and so they are full and overflowing. For in that simplicity, the spirit finds itself united with God without means; and this union, with the exercise which belongs to it, shall endure eternally, as I have told you heretofore.

Experiences with John of Ruysbroeck

"*The love of Jesus is at once avid and generous. All that He has, all that He is, He gives; all that we are, all that we have, He takes.*"

&

"*Contemplation places us in a purity and radiance which is far above our understanding.*"

John of Ruysbroeck

John has many diagrams to explain his view and understanding of the trinity and how the divinity of God could be explained without trying to remove the mystery.

The spiritual experience with the divine Godhead is difficult to communicate in language that seeks to define when what is needed is more loose definitions. The eloquence of human language is lacking in its ability to paint a picture. Most communication in heaven happens with light, the communication with light, transfers the information much quicker, and helps complex content to be placed into visual images.

The trinitarian concept can be quite complicated, In the diagrams below, I try to draw some images and take from existing symbolism to discuss the topic and make it easier to comprehend.

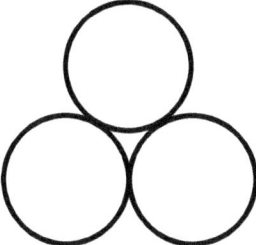

The basis of our understanding of the trinity is that God has three personalities in one unit, and through these "Personalities" we can encounter the divine in Christianity. God is both Father (ABBA), Son (Jesus Christ) and Holy Spirit.

Although the word trinity is not in the bible, it is clearly understood and undergirding the principles in the bible, when Jesus says. "I do everything I see my Father is doing", Jesus is busy elevating the Father (Abba).

This theme is seen in the whole scripture, Jesus says again "If you have seen Me, you have seen the Father in heaven", trying to explain there is no difference in divinity, only a difference in function.

This idea is also seen when discussing the Holy Spirit; Jesus says, "it is better for me to leave, so that the Spirit may come".

Moving onto the second diagram it shows where the interlinking of Jesus, Abba, and Holy Spirit is, trying to describe the union and the separation at the same time, one-unit functioning in three parts.

In heaven this realm of understanding is a dimension of frequency, energy and color, when one experiences this realm, one understands this is not the highest heaven, it is still a place of creation, where unity is being explored, and revealed. In this place in the kingdom realms of God, we understand that God is functioning in unity, there is communication, there is relationship, and there is a commonality of being.

It is often explained that there can be no unity without diversity, in this place, God is till expressing His divine diversity, yet also showing complete unity, unity of purpose, unity of understanding, and most importantly instant, completely understood communication.

The next diagram is an understanding beyond energies and human concepts, is the realm of the One. The Hebrew word is "Echad." This is the place where we pray "Behold oh Israel, the Lord your God is One God."

The personalities of God become intertwined, and the "Oneness" is more expressed, this is also the place where mystics experience this union, a place where we are pulled into the trinitary love dance, and shows how in the Oneness there is no separation.

In this place we understand that God is "Ayin Sof" or "Ayin Or"; as I read how Jan Ruysbrook tried to explain this place, and then saw how he took me into this place, where there is no space, no time, no light – just being.

The place of existence, only consciousness and perception, where God is the only driver of the experience, in other dimensions, the virtues or human capabilities are still used to understand, to comprehend this place. In this dimension that is not the case, there is no human ability to drive the experience, God becomes the driver, He is in sole control of the whole experience and even the ability to get understanding is only found in a deep sense of abiding.

Once the "soul" accesses the lower dimensions, this reality fades slowly, and then, when the soul re-awakens by the divine hand, the remembrance of this place is again perceived.

The fourth diagram shows the "outside" part of God. In this place, God is beyond all creation, God is in a sense outside of us. God will in some way always be beyond humanity, there is a place in existence, where God is bigger and exists in a realm beyond everything that has ever been created.

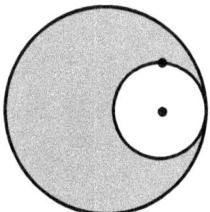

The Creator of an object can certainly not be limited by His own creation, to be Creator God, there is a place where only God exists, and nothing else, just Him.

I know these are tough concepts to convey, yet I also understand they are important because our current society is moving from a many persona type culture to a "one-ness" concept of God. We are moving from individualism to a more globalist perspective on the world, we are all connected via one large data and information highway.

This concept is now moving from globalism to universalism, which is where the problem starts occurring, if we experience union with God, we start seeing God in everything, and every person we meet. Nature and all of creation is not excluded from God. Everything is included in God, as some would say "He is the All in All", however, if we miss this 4th diagram, our understanding will be based on no-separation theology, which excludes the real hidden truth.

God is outside of everything, all the time, yet God is incarnational based on the finished work of Jesus. The incarnation reality of God, in the human flesh, cannot supersede this reality, that we are not God, only God is God, and thus separation is the only, highest reality of God, but this separation is one of existence and not of being.

God is always present with us, yet we are not always present with God. Where humanity and creation do not exist, God still exists. In this Theology of Epistemology, we know that we can only know to a point, the very fact that we know something, means there is a place where we don't know anything. The very existence of God is predicated on the idea that God is on some level un-knowable, otherwise, God would not be God.

QUESTIONS

1. Which part of his life, is similar to your own life?

2. From the extracts of his writing which part did you enjoy the most?

3. Could it be possible that no matter which time we live in history, we share some human struggles?

4. Have you ever thought about your ideas about God?

5. Do you think Theology has an impact on how we interpret reality, and the future?

CHAPTER 10
Saint Francis de Sales

"Make friends with the angels, who though invisible are always with you. Often invoke them, constantly praise them, and make good use of their help and assistance in all your temporal and spiritual affairs." – Saint Francis de Sales

CHAPTER 10 – Saint Francis de Sales

Born:	21 August 1567
Died:	28 December 1622
Nationality:	French
Location:	Lyon France
Outlook:	Catholic
Scribe:	Jane Frances de Chantal
Books:	Introduction to the Devout Life
	Treatise on the Love of God
	Letters of Spiritual Direction
Interests:	Theologian, Mystic, Writer
Achievements:	Doctor of the Church
Key Teachings:	Heart of Jesus, Crown of Thorns
Beatified:	8 January 1661
Canonized:	8 April 1665

Introduction to Saint Francis de Sales

"Half an hour's meditation each day is essential, except when you are busy. Then a full hour is needed."

Saint Francis de Sales

Francis de Sales was born on 21 August 1567, to the Nobel Sales family in Haute-Savoie, France.

His mother was the only child of a French magistrate, and his father Francois de Sales was the Lord of Boisy. His father was grooming him in the legal profession. He was educated in La Roche-Sur-Foron, and at the age of eight at the Capuchin College in Annecy.

In 1583 Francis then 16, went to the Collège de Clermont in Paris, to study the humanities. Francis was educated in all the social graces, like fencing and dancing, a typical tall, dark and handsome young man. In 1587 after a prolonged time of spiritual awakening, as a result of hearing a French preacher, he prayed to the black Madonna, and dedicated his life to divine service. He became a tertiary in the Minim Order.

In 1588 he went on to study Theology and law at the University of Padua in Italy where he received the priest Antonio Possevino as his confessor and mentor.

He was ordained a provost in 1593, after receiving his doctorate, in the chapter of Geneva, he was ordained by Claude de Granier the bishop of Geneva.

Francis embarked on many fervent campaigns of evangelism, almost Calvinist in his approach, despite his efforts, he met with great opposition in Thonon, where he survived several attempts on his life, due to his efforts. After traveling to Rome and Paris, and meeting with Pope Clement VIII and Henry IV of France, he made some alliances with them.

In 1599 he was appointed the Bishop of Geneva, and in 1601, he was sent on a diplomatic assignment to Henry IV. The king was known for his liberal morality, however Francis de Sales, received favour with the king, due to his gentle manner, and learned demeanor. He also advised Cardinal Berulle and Madame Acarie about the Carmelite order introduction to France.

In 1602 Francis de Sales was ordained the bishop of Geneva, although he stayed in Annecy, France, due to the Calvinist occupation of Geneva.

Francis was known as an orator, and those under his care, both clergy and laity were well-educated and versed in the scriptures, this was uncommon in the era. In 1606 he founded a women's order, "Order of the visitation of Holy Mary" which required their nuns to remain cloistered lives.

In 1622 Francis traveled to Lyon in France, on tour with the Duke of Savoy, he died in Lyon, after suffering a stroke while on tour with the Duke.

Theology and Doctrine of Francis de Sales

Introduction to the Devout Life – Page 38, on Mental Prayer

I commend earnest mental prayer to you, more particularly such as bears upon the Life and Passion of our Lord. If you contemplate Him frequently in meditation, your whole soul will be filled with Him, you will grow in His Likeness, and your actions will be moulded on His. He is the Light of the world; therefore in Him, by Him, and for Him we shall be enlightened and illuminated; He is the Tree of Life, beneath the shadow of which we must find rest;—He is the Living Fountain of Jacob's well, wherein we may wash away every stain. Children learn to speak by hearing their mother talk, and stammering forth their childish sounds in imitation; and so if we cleave to the Savior in meditation, listening to His words, watching His actions and intentions, we shall learn in time, through His Grace, to speak, act and will like Himself.

Introduction to the Devout Life – Page 44

But your resolutions must be made after the affections, and quite at the end of your meditation, and that all the more because in these you must enter upon ordinary familiar subjects and things which would be liable to cause distractions if they were intruded among your spiritual affections.

Amid your affections and resolutions it is well occasionally to make use of colloquies, and to speak sometimes to your Lord, sometimes to your guardian Angel, or to those persons who are concerned in the mystery you are meditating, to the Saints, to yourself, your own heart, to sinners, and even to the inanimate creation around, as David so often does in the Psalms, as well as other Saints in their meditations and prayers.

Introduction to the Devout Life – Page 45, 5 Shorter Kinds of Prayer

BESIDES your systematic meditation and your other vocal prayers, there are five shorter kinds of prayer, which are as aids and assistants to the great devotion, and foremost among these is your morning prayer, as a general preparation for all the day's work. It should be made in this wise.

1. Thank God, and adore Him for His Grace which has kept you safely through the night, and if in anything you have offended against Him, ask forgiveness.

2. Call to mind that the day now beginning is given you in order that you may work for Eternity, and make a stedfast resolution to use this day for that end.

3. Consider beforehand what occupations, duties and occasions are likely this day to enable you to serve God

4. Next, humble yourself before God, confessing that of yourself you could carry out nothing that you have planned, either in avoiding evil or seeking good.

Treatise on the Love of God – Page 78, First Book: The Divine Love

For thus, to make divine love live and reign in us, we kill self-love, and if we cannot entirely annihilate it at least we weaken it in such a way that though it lives yet it does not reign in us. As, on the contrary, in forsaking divine love we may adhere to that of creatures, which is the infamous adultery with which the Divine lover so often reproaches sinners.

Treatise on the Love of God – Page 78, First Book: The Divine Love

Basil, rosemary, marigold, hyssop, cloves, chamomile, nutmeg, lemon, and musk, put together and incorporated, yield a truly delightful odour by the mixture of their good perfume; yet not nearly so much as does the water which is distilled from them, in which the sweets of all these ingredients separated from their bodies are mingled in a much more excellent manner, uniting in a most perfect scent, which penetrates the sense of smelling far more strongly than it would do if with it and its water the bodies of the ingredients were found mingled and united. So love may be found in the unions proper to the sensual powers, mixed with the unions of intellectual powers, but never so excellently as when the spirits and souls alone, separated from all corporeal affections but united together, make love pure and spiritual. For the scent of affections thus mingled is not only sweeter and better, but more lively, more active and more essential.

Treatise on the Love of God – Page 81, First Book: The Divine Love

Our reason, or, to speak better, our soul in so far as it is reasonable, is the true temple of the great God, who there takes up his chief residence. "I sought thee," says S. Augustine, "outside myself, but I found thee not, because thou art within me." In this mystical temple there are also three courts, which are three different degrees of reason; in the first we reason according to the experience of sense, in the second according to human sciences, in the third according to faith: and in fine, beyond this, there is a certain eminence or supreme point of the reason and spiritual faculty, which is not guided by the light of argument or reasoning, but by a simple view of the understanding and a simple movement of the will, by which the spirit bends and submits to the truth and the will of God.

Treatise on the Love of God – Page 102, Second Book: The Divine Love

Saviour's redemption is applied to us in as many different manners as there are souls, yet still, love is the universal means of salvation which mingles with everything, and without which nothing is profitable, as we shall show elsewhere. The Cherubim were placed at the gate of the earthly paradise with their flaming sword, to teach us that no one shall enter into the heavenly paradise who is not pierced through with the sword of love. For this cause, Theotimus, the sweet Jesus who bought us with his blood, is infinitely desirous that we should love him that we may eternally be saved, and desires we may be saved that we may love him eternally, his love tending to our salvation and our salvation to his love

Treatise on the Love of God – Page 111, Second Book: The Divine Love

Even so, my dear Theotimus, when the inspiration, as a sacred gale, comes to blow us forward into the air of holy love, it first takes our will, and by the sentiment of some heavenly delectation it moves it, extending and unfolding the natural inclination which the will has to good, so that this same inclination serves as a hold by which to seize our spirit. And all this, as I have said, is done in us without us, for it is the divine favour that prevents us in this sort. But if our will thus holily prevented, perceiving the wings of her inclination moved, displayed, extended, stirred, and agitated, by this heavenly wind, contributes, be it never so little, its consent—Ah! how happy it is, Theotimus. The same favourable inspiration which has seized us, mingling its action with our consent, animating our feeble motions with its vigour, and vivifying our weak cooperation by the power of its operation, will aid, conduct, and accompany us, from love to love, even unto the act of most holy faith requisite for our conversion.

True God! Theotimus, what a consolation it is to consider the secret method by which the Holy Ghost pours into our hearts the first rays and feelings of his light and vital heat! O Jesus! how delightful a pleasure it is to see celestial love.

Treatise on the Love of God – Page 123, Second Book: The Divine Love

Thus the famous penitent lover first loved her Saviour, her love was converted into tears, and these tears into an excellent love; whence Our Saviour told her that many sins were pardoned her because she had loved much.115 And as we see fire turns wine into a certain water which is called almost everywhere aquavitæ, which so easily takes and augments fire that in many places it is also termed ardent; so the amorous consideration of the goodness which, while it ought to have been sovereignly loved, has been offended by sin, produces the water of holy penitence; and from this water the fire of divine love issues, thence properly termed water of life or ardent.

Treatise on the Love of God – Page 184, Fifth Book: The Divine Love

God being replenished with a goodness which surpasses all praise and honour, receives no advantage nor increase by all the benedictions which we give him. He is neither richer nor greater, nor more content or happy by them, for his happiness, his content, his greatness, and his riches neither are nor can be any other thing than the divine infinity of his goodness. At the same time, since, according to our ordinary estimation, honour is held one of the greatest effects of our benevolence towards others, and since by it we not only do not imply any indigence in those we honour, but rather protest that they abound in excellence, we therefore make use of this kind of benevolence towards God, who not only approves it, but exacts it, as suitable to our condition, and so proper to testify the respectful love we bear him, that he has ordained we should render and refer all honour and glory unto him.

Treatise on the Love of God – Page 196, Sixth Book: The Divine Love – Mystical Theology

Theotimus, how the silence of afflicted lovers speaks by the apple of their eye, and by tears? Truly the chief exercise in mystical theology is to speak to God and to hear God speak in the bottom of the heart; and because this discourse passes in most secret aspirations and inspirations, we term it a silent conversing. Eyes speak to eyes, and heart to heart, and none understand what passes save the sacred lovers who speak.

Treatise on the Love of God – Page 198, Sixth Book: The Divine Love – Mystical Theology

Such is the devout soul in meditation. She passes from mystery to mystery, not at random, or only to solace herself in viewing the admirable beauty of those divine objects, but deliberately and of set purpose, to find out motives of love or of some heavenly affection; and having found them she draws them to her, she relishes them, she loads herself with them, and having brought them back and put them within her heart, she lays up what she sees most useful for her advancement, by finally making resolutions suitable for the time of temptation. Thus in the Canticle of Canticles the heavenly spouse, as a mystical bee, settles, now on the eyes, now on the lips, on the cheeks, on the hair of her beloved, to draw thence the sweetness of a thousand passions of love, noting in particular whatever she finds best for this. So that, inflamed with holy love, she speaks with him, she questions him, she listens to him, sighs, aspires, admires him, as he on his part fills her with delight, inspiring her, touching and opening her heart, and pouring into it brightness, lights and sweetnesses without end, but in so secret a manner that one may rightly say of this holy conversation of the soul with God, what the holy text says of God's with Moses: that Moses being alone upon the top of the mountain spoke to God, and God answered him.

Treatise on the Love of God – Page 231, Sixth Book: The Divine Love – Mystical Theology

AN ecstasy is called a rapture inasmuch as God does thereby rapt us, and raise us up to himself, and a rapture is termed an ecstasy, because by it we go and remain out of, and above, ourselves, to be united to God. And although the attractions by which God draws us be admirably pleasing, sweet and delicious, yet on account of the force which the divine beauty and goodness have to draw unto them the attention and application of the spirit, it seems that it not only raises us but that it ravishes and bears us away.

Treatise on the Love of God – Page 253, Sixth Book: The Divine Love – Mystical Theology

God wills that we should believe, the goods he will have us hope for, the pains he will have us dread, what he will have us love, the commandments he will have us observe, and the counsels he desires us to follow. And this is called God's signified will, because he has signified and made manifest unto us that it is his will and intention that all this should be believed, hoped for, feared, loved and practised.

Now forasmuch as this signified will of God proceeds by way of desire, and not by way of absolute will, we have power either to follow it by obedience, or by disobedience to resist it; for to this purpose God makes three acts of his will: he wills that we should be able to resist, he desires that we should not resist, and yet allows us to resist if we please. That we have power to resist depends on our natural condition and liberty; that we do resist proceeds from our malice; that we do not resist is according to the desire of the divine goodness. And therefore when we resist, God contributes nothing to our disobedience, but leaving our will in the hands of its liberty permits it to make choice of evil; but when we obey, God contributes his assistance, his inspiration, and his grace.

Treatise on the Love of God – Page 349, Sixth Book: The Divine Love – Mystical Theology

Charity is then the bond of perfection, since in it all the perfections of the soul are contained and assembled, and since without it, not only can one not have the whole array of virtues, but one cannot even have the perfection of any virtue. Without the cement and mortar which fasten the stones and walls, the whole edifice goes to rack; were it not for the nerves, muscles and sinews, the whole body would be undone; and without charity the virtues can never sustain one another.

Treatise on the Love of God – Page 361, Sixth Book: The Divine Love – Mystical Theology

Now they are not only inseparable from charity, but, all things well considered, and speaking precisely, they are the principal virtues, properties and qualities of charity. For Wisdom is in fact no other thing than the love which relishes, tastes and experiences, how sweet and delicious God is;. Understanding is nothing else than love attentive to consider and penetrate the beauty of the truths of faith, to know thereby God in himself, and then descending from this to consider him in creatures; Science, on the other hand, is but the same love, keeping us attentive to the knowledge of ourselves and creatures, to make us reascend to a more perfect knowledge of the service which we owe to God;. Counsel is also love, insomuch as it makes us careful, attentive, and wise in choosing the means proper to serve God holily.

Personal Journey with Saint Francis de Sales

Meeting Francis was like meeting a professor and a scientist at once, he clearly wanted to understand the underlying nature of the world, not just the consequences but the causes.

I could see the curiosity in his eyes, and the complete delight in details, the small mechanics of the world around us, others would easily gloss over, he would regard with a sense of complete wonder.

He started explaining the throne room of God, and trying to help me decipher some of the hidden mysteries of God, hidden in plain sight, both in scripture and while standing before God in heaven.

When we enter the throne room of God, we are faced with an unknown world of wonders, where it seems as though the very essence of the place is speaking and declaring the greatness of God. Then you look at the throne and you are once again astounded by the brilliance of it all.

I have always been fascinated by the wheels around the throne, and the wheels within the wheels as Ezekiel explains in the bible. So, I was excited when engaging Francis, this was the very thing that he wanted to share with me.

He explained that the wheels of the throne, signified the dimensions and metron of God's eternal government. We see the wheels of the throne as a way for God "drive" the throne! However, it is only a metaphor for the all-encompassing and every changing nature of God's government in creation.

The wheels keep on moving, as if moving by themselves, the very nature of God animates all movement, all existence, God is every force which enables the atomic structure of the creation to remain in suspension.

We would like to discover the "God" particle; however, this particle is ever-moving, ever-changing and always in a constant state of flux or fluid movement. The fluidity of God's government displayed in creation, can look like wheels or elliptical patterns, like the movement of stars or the patterns of planets in the cosmic dance of creation.

The cyclic nature of creation creates the illusion of movement; however, the movement is only observable from a single point, a point which is in itself, moving.

Francis commented that our modern understanding of propulsion will at some stage come to a place where we will need to understand a complete still point, or what some scientists have called Zero-Point Energy.

The fractional understanding of this zero point becomes the issue, as the vibrational situation of creation creates a permanent movement, an ever-increasing shaking, and this movement then aligns the creation to the "plumb-line" of creation, the original intention of God in creation, the "anima" as Jung would call this principle.

The only two times in creation when darkness enveloped all existence were when the lamb was slain before the foundation, and the multiverse emanated from this place, and the moment Jesus died on the cross, the complete darkness signified a complete reboot of the system.

A systemic shift into a dimensional plane, in a sense a time rift which created endless new possibilities, birthed out of the very depths of Gods nature, in the heart of God, or the mind of God, since God has no anatomy to speak of, the moment of crucifixion became a fulcrum of divine destiny.

All the wheels in the throne room pivot from this place of inertia and build a systemic reality which then enables God to manifest His desires on the earth, and elsewhere in creation. The movement of the eyes of the wheels, then observes the change, thereby creating an observant point, which structures, the place of creation into materiality.

The double slit experiment proves that observation changes reality, and in this case, the observer being the eyes of the wheels, under the throne of God, magnifies and solidifies the matrix of creation, to build a stable platform, for the thoughts of God, to be bought into creation.

In some sense, God is always and eternally creating, from the point of the sacrifice of Jesus even now.

The Ophanim wheels under the throne of God, is not just points of observation, causing the manifestation, but also power generating systems, that create with movement, the rotation of the wheels in every direction and dimension, is not there to build momentum, they also create energetic systems which are used to sustain creation.

God does not need to really move the way we think, God is already omnipresent, meaning that God is already everywhere present. In the Throne room dimension, this is then a place where the dominion of God is expressed in a spiritual metaphor.

Francis wanted me to understand how the throne of God operates, as the changes in humanity and the coming developments in energy and vibrational frequency will all be based on the structures of the Throne room of God. God created us to rule creation, which means that we will also need to understand the angelic structures of dominion, and would be expected of the " sons" of God to rule the way God rules creation.

QUESTIONS

1. Which part of his life challenged you the most?

2. Which part of the extracts did you like, is there any part you disagree with his ideas?

3. What part does prayer play in our thoughts and theology?

4. Is God's Throne room accessible to you today?

5. Does the throne room of God change as we move in history?

6. Is there only one throne in heaven?

CHAPTER 11
Saint Patrick of Ireland

"[God] watched over me before I knew him, and before I learned sense or even distinguished between good and evil, and he protected me, and consoled me as a father would his son." - Saint Patrick

Born:	400AD
Died:	471AD
Nationality:	Ireland
Location:	Armagh
Outlook:	Celtic Catholic Mystic
Interests:	Monastic Life, Nature
Achievements:	300 Churches, over 100,000 Irish Baptized
Key Teachings:	Care for the Poor, The Way of Monastic Prayer,
Supernatural Miracles:	Turning water into beer, weather miracles, many healing miracles

The Life of Saint Patrick of Ireland

Patrick was born in the fourth century. His father was Calpurnius, a Roman, who held a military position in the army of Rome and his mother, Conchessa, a close relative to St Martin of Tours.

Born into a noble British family and Roman citizen, Patrick was able to get an education. Patrick's family was quite large, he had one brother and five sisters.

At the age of 16 he was kidnapped by Irish pirates, and enslaved for 6 years, he spent this time as a shepherd, and converted to Christianity during this dark time in his life.

Patrick was able to escape the enslavement; he walked to a port city 200 miles away and found a ship Captain he could convince to take him to Britain. He had walked for 28 days in the wild lowlands of Britain before he was able to find his family again, now in his early twenties.

After returning home to his family, Patrick left Britain for France where he studied at Auxerre, he was ordained into the priesthood by Saint Germanus of Auxerre.

Patrick had a vision that influenced his decision to return to his homeland in Ireland to preach the gospel. He landed at Wicklow by ship, however after a cold reception, he proceeded to the County Meath where he met Benignus, the son of the chieftain Secsnen, who then joined Patrick as a disciple.

Ireland was not hospitable to strangers, and although Patrick had huge success converting thousands of people, baptizing them, and dealing with the chieftains and kings, his unwillingness to accept any gifts from the kings, made his relationship with the ruling class of Ireland difficult.

Patrick had many noble females converted, and he also dealt with the sons of kings, often converting them from their native pagan beliefs.

Patrick died on 471 AD at Dichu's Barn, on Strangford Lough.

Theology of Saint Patrick of Ireland.

The Theology of Patrick is an early Celtic theology. Although Patrick has been used by many people for political and ecclesiastical gain, it is important to note his life, and memory and his treasure for humanity, was always his commitment to see the Irish nation change from "pagans" to Christians.

He did not see this progression, as a conversion, but a natural progression, from men looking at nature, like Paul says, to men who meet the very God they have been looking for before. The Celtic Christian way is not a protestant or Catholic way, it is the way God intended it to be, that is why he sent this man, a man who loved nature, loved Ireland, but above all loved God.

Breastplate of Saint Patrick – Stanza 8-9 of the Hymn

Christ with me, Christ before me,

Christ behind me, Christ within me,

Christ beneath me, Christ above me,

Christ at my right, Christ at my left,

Christ in breadth, Christ in length,

Christ in height.

Christ in the heart of every man who thinks of me,

Christ in the mouth of every man who speaks to me,

Christ in the eye of every man that sees me,

Christ in the ear of every man that hears me.

The Confession – Page 43, Patrick Preaches and Baptizes at his own cost

But perhaps, since I have baptized so many thousand men, I might have

from some of them? Tell it to me, and I will Or when the Lord ordained everywhere clergy, through my humble ministry, I dispensed the rite gratuitously. If I asked of any of them even the price of my shoe, tell it against me, and I will restore you more. I spent for you, that they might

receive me; and among you, and everywhere, I traveled for your sake, amid many perils, even to remote places, where there was no one beyond, and where no one else had ever penetrated—to baptize or ordain clergy, or to confirm the people. The Lord granting it, I diligently and most cheerfully, for your salvation, defrayed all things. During this time I gave presents to expected half a screpall restore it to you, the kings; nevertheless they seized me"

The Confession – Page 43, Patrick Preaches and Baptizes at his own cost

Not my grace, but God, indeed, hath put this desire into my heart, that I should be one of the hunters or fishers, whom of old God promised before in the last days. I am envied. What shall I do, Lord? I am greatly despised. Behold! Thy sheep are torn around me, and are plundered even

by the above-mentioned robbers, by the order of Coroticus, with hostile

mind. Far from the love of God is the betrayer of the Christians into the

hands of Scots and Picts! Ravening wolves have swallowed up the flock of the Lord,

which everywhere in Ireland was increasing with the greatest

diligence; and the sons of the Scots and the daughters of princes are monks

and virgins of Christ (in numbers) I cannot enumerate.

Proverbs of Patrick – Page 54, Some extracts about Judgement

"*Judges of the Church ought not to be so swift in judgment until they know how too true it may be which is written, 'Do not desire quickly to be a judge.'*"

"*Judges of the Church ought to 'judge just judgment,' 'for with whatever judgment they shall judge, it shall be judged to them.'*"

"*Patrick says: 'Look into the examples of the elders, where you will find no guile.'*"

Miracle Accounts of Saint Patrick

The Druid's Defeat – Page 60, Celtic Flame

After a formal greeting between Laeghaire and Patrick, the wizard Lochru attached him angrily with contention and shouting. He became malicious and hostile and even violent, blaspheming the Holy Trinity. Patrick's anger was roused and he called upon God, "O Lord, Who can do all things and on Whose power everything depends. You have sent us here to preach Your Name to the heathen. Now let this ungodly man, who blasphemes Your Name, be lifted up and let him die."

No sooner had Patrick finished speaking than a super-natural force raised the wizard in the air. He fell heavily down, his head striking a stone. And so he died in the pres- ence of those assembled.

The heathen, seeing their own subdued and realizing that Patrick had more power than the druids, were greatly affected. But the king was enraged at the fate of Lochru, on whom he had depended. He then wanted to take the life of Patrick.

"Slay this man," he cried to his guards.

But Patrick stood firmly in his place. With flashing eyes and resonant voice he said, "Let God arise and His enemies be scattered. Let them that hate Him, flee from before His face! As smoke vanished, so let them vanish away: as wax melts before the fire, so let the wicked perish at the presence of God."

Patrick's Challenge

The king, hearing of St. Patrick's arrival, greatly rejoiced and asked him to come in to where his two children lay dead. He then promised, before all those present, that if God restored his children to life, he and all the citizens would become Christians. Seeing such a gain of souls in the sight of the king, his nobles, and all the common people, Patrick raised from death to life those princely children. Their bodily resurrection attributed greatly toward the spiritual resurrection of their father and the rest of his people. The king and all his subjects, being astonished at this great miracle, turned away from the worship of idols and they were baptized in the spring.

From that day the king and all the people worshiped God and gave liberally to Patrick, so that he was able to give to the poor in that place and other places and have enough to build churches.

(Ref. Ecclesiastical History of Ireland, Rev. Dr. Lanigan. Sexta Vita S. Patricii, Joycelin notes.)

Patrick's Prayers For Ireland – Page 69, Celtic Flame

Patrick went to a high mountain in the range of Mayo in order to seek god and to fast and pray. For forty days he fasted with watching and prayers and travail. Toward the end of the fast, the mountain was surrounded by many demons in the form of large black birds, screaming and giv- ing off a *foul smell. Patrick continued singing psalms and hymns to no avail. Finally Patrick threw his bell at the birds and commanded them to leave. They left and immediately he was surrounded by an angelic choir. Also the angel who was always Patrick's companion, Victor, came and said, "Everything you select shall be yours; every land—both hills and valleys, glens and woods. Every petition shall be granted."*

Patrick's first petition was that every Irish man, woman and child would have opportunity to hear the Gospel and secondly, that barbarian invaders should not prevail against the Irish people. Victor commanded Patrick to get down from the mountain but Patrick refused until every petition he asked was granted. Patrick continued to ask for many blessings for Ireland.

My Experience with Saint Patrick of Ireland

Patrick walked into the realm I was standing in, with a very soft regal nature, it's almost as though he felt the cloak or monk's tunic was the way he is, not fancy not trying to be somebody special, it was his way, a man of the earth, a man without the need to display authority.

He started discussing our need to take responsibility for the earth. This is not just a responsibility we carry like worshiping the earth, we don't worship an earth goddess, God gave the earth to Adam/man, if we will become mature, part of our responsibility will be to act like Adam acted before the fall.

Patrick explained that Adam understood the earth, like a chemist understands the reactions of certain chemicals mixing, and the effect they have on each other. He understood this due to his divine nature God created him with, his access to this understanding, helped him frame the animals into materiality, and helped him name the very creation God intended for the earth. Adam understood the blueprint of the earth on a deeply emotional, spiritual, and intellectual level.

Patrick commented that if we believe humanity will come into maturity of sonship, our way of dealing with the earth will need to change. We can't see the earth as a mechanistic system, which was created just to resource humanity. The Garden God created for Adam, was the unique habitat Adam also needed to flourish.

Humanity would need to come to a place of understanding the earth has an impact on our health systems, our conscious awareness, and the very nature of our Experience of God. Our connectedness to nature brings the reality of the spiritual into materiality.

In the past, due to the Industrial Revolution our theology did not include the earth. We wanted to save souls and change the world, but we never thought about the whole earth, we only counted the human soul. I am proposing that we as a species need to learn to honor what the Father has given us. Part of maturity is having respect for the things you are given and building a better system for your species.

Yes, the bible does say we will be given a new earth, and a new heaven, maybe the new earth will depend on those who have a new thinking system. If we are given a new earth today, we will pollute and corrupt the earth to the same level we have today.

When Paul writes all creation speaks of the Gospel and preaches about the existence of God, the nature of creation is the very nature of God. A system of constant rejuvenation and restoration of the old, into the new. If we believe God will just come down to the earth, and fix the mess we made, we are still immature sons, always asking the Father of Heaven to take responsibility for the earth, He intended for man from the first day of creation.

If creation speaks of God's glory, and we silence the voice of nature, what does that mean, what are we actually doing, we are silencing the worship of creation, and creating a system of silence, where nothing can testify of God.

If the very rocks will cry out, that means the vibrational frequency of creation worships God on a quantum level, since He is the one holding the whole creation together by His divine word. If we silence the divine harmony of creation, if the symphony of nature is silenced by humanity, the very nature of humanity will change.

We all know what happens to creatures once we remove them from the wild, once we remove their natural habitat and force them into confinement, their whole demure changes, even their procreation becomes an issue, independent from their diet.

In the future, societies will look back on our day, a day of fossil fuel and pollution, consumerism and judge us based on our backward spending and consumption patterns. The church does not need to be the last guest at the party. God expects us to be the voice of the Holy Spirit speaking, restoring and bringing life to creation.

The doctrine of immortality cannot just be a doctrine for humanity; we will at some stage be challenged to with deal the spirit of Death. Death is our final enemy, and if creation, the sons of Christ are not subject to mortality, neither does their world have to bow the knee to the spirit of death. Jesus was able to get the keys to the kingdom and the keys to death. If Jesus has these keys, only those who know the master Jesus, will be able to ask him to release immortal, eternal sons into the earth.

If all creation groans, it groans not just for the revealing of the sons, to glorification of the sons, but that the Glory of the Lord may be seen in the land of the living, all things becoming living. This might depend on creation responding to Jesus inside the sons. There will be those who choose to remain as they are, who prefer their disfiguration of mortality to the transfiguration of Jesus in the life of the earth.

There will be a day Patrick said, where the Saints will walk with the sons, and the angels will walk men and women who love God, the earth will once again be multi-dimensional, multi-faceted, and like a diamond in the Crown of Jesus, the earth will shine His glory into every galaxy and solar system.

The nations will come to the brightness of your shining, as they see the glory of the Lord, being inter-dimensionally displayed on the sons of Righteousness. The royal diadem will shine once again, and full access will be granted into the heavens again, hence a new heaven, structured like the garden before, where the energetic systems of the earth will change completely.

Visible and invisible will merge like waterfalls and will no longer be divisible the way you have chosen to do so now. The nature of God might never be completely displayed like we would now have words to describe the revealing, but the revealing of the sons, will not be the revealing of the Father. The Father chose not to reveal Himself but through His Son, Jesus, in future, only the sons will be revealed, and their nature will be the full stature of the head Christ Jesus, they will reveal Him, as He reveals the Father, who chooses the un-revealed secrecy of mystery, to sustain the divine darkness, the cloud of unknowing, the place unsearchable by all the created ones.

QUESTIONS

1. Which part of his life inspires you?
2. Which of his miracles are hard to believe?
3. Do you think the environment is important to believers if God is going to give us a new earth?
4. If we are custodians of the earth, having dominion over creation, does the state of creation reflect our condition?
5. Do you think Celtic thinking could still impact us today?
6. Is there hope for this generation, if Jesus does not come in 40 years?

CHAPTER 12
Meister Eckhart

"A just person is one who is conformed and transformed into justice." – Meister Eckhart

CHAPTER 12 - Meister Eckhart

Born:	1260
Died:	1328
Nationality:	Flemish
Location:	Avignon France
Outlook:	Catholic, Dominican Order
Interests:	Theology, Prayer, Mystic, Author, Philosopher
Achievements:	Reformation of the church theology
Key Teachings:	Neo-Platonism

Books:

Paradise of the Intelligent Soul/Paradise of the Intellectual Soul

The Book of the Divine Consolation

Counsels on Discernment/Discourses on Instruction/Talks of Instruction

The Life of Meister Eckhart

"A human being has so many skins inside, covering the depths of the heart. We know so many things, but we don't know ourselves! Why, thirty or forty skins or hides, as thick and hard as an ox's or bear's, cover the soul. Go into your own ground and learn to know yourself there."

Meister Eckhart

Eckhart von Hochheim was born in Tambach in Germany in 1260 AD. He joined the Dominican Order at Erfurt when he was 15 years old. Not much information exists about his earlier childhood.

He studied in Cologne at the age of 18, and it appears as if he also studied at the University of Paris around this time, however, details are very scarce.

In 1293 he was appointed as Lecturer at the Dominican Convent of St. Jacques in Paris. While there he lectured for Peter Lombard on the "Sentences." In 1294 he was appointed as the Prior to Erfurt and Provincial of Thuringia, where he wrote his first German work, Reden der Unterweisung (The Talks of Instructions/Counsels on Discernment).

He then became the Provincial for Saxony in 1303, this province stretched from the Netherlands to Latvia. He had to serve 47 convents in the province. In 1304 the General Aymeric of Piacenza appointed him as Vicar-General for Bohemia. Eckhart served the Provincial of Saxony until 1311.

In May 1311 Eckhart was appointed as a teacher in Paris, he only lectured for 2 academic years. He then spent some time in Strasbourg, preaching to Dominicans. In 1324 Eckhart left and went to the Dominican house in Cologne, where he preached and taught.

Eckhart was a very controversial figure in the church; he had various theological critics and opponents to his ideas and interpretation of scripture. In 1327, he was asked to Avignon to defend himself in the inquisition, before Pope John XXII. Of his 150 articles, only 28 were found to be suspect.

Meister Eckhart died on 28 January 1328, before the verdict could be made known at his inquisition. Pope John XXII only condemned some of the articles as heretical, however, there was no verdict upon Eckhart as a heretic.

Currently, the church denies any sentence against Eckhart and supports his theology, however, due to a lack of surviving manuscripts, the 28 original documents in question, the church believes Eckhart was taken out of context.

Ideas of Meister Eckhart

The four-fold path of the creation spiritual tradition can be summarized in the following manner:

1. Via Positiva. (Positive Way)
2. Via Negativa. (Negative Way)
3. Via Creativa. (Creative Way)
4. Via Transformativa. (Transformative Way)

Meister Eckhart was a very controversial figure in respect to his theology, and his understanding and interpretation of scripture. Although becoming more popular in some movements today, linked to other faiths like Buddhism, I believe his thoughts are profoundly Christian in nature.

Although the church still does not agree with all his views, much of his theology would sound common place to the modern ear.

His biggest problem was in the descriptions of his theology, many later followers tried to interpret his works and give some clarity regarding his views. This has been done with some success in the west.

Sermon 2 – Page 40, Mystical works of Meister Eckhart

Now note the answer. It is a property of this birth that it always comes with fresh light. It always brings a great light to the soul, for it is the nature of good to diffuse itself wherever it is. In this birth God streams into the soul in such abundance of light, so flooding the essence and ground of the soul that it runs over and floods into the powers and into the outward man. Thus it befell Paul when on his journey God touched him with His light and spoke to him: a reflection of the light shone outwardly, so that his companions saw it surrounding Paul like the blessed (in heaven). The superfluity of light in the ground of the soul wells over into the body which is filled with radiance. No sinner can receive this light, nor is he worthy to, being full of sin and wickedness, which is called 'darkness.'

Sermon 3 - Page 48, Mystical works of Meister Eckhart

Though there is motion, yet it is all one; it comes from one end, which is God, and returns to the same, as if I were to go from one end of this house to the other; that would indeed be motion, but only of one in the same. Thus too, in this activity, we remain in a state of contemplation in God. The one rests in the other, and perfects the other. For God's purpose in the union of contemplation is fruitfulness in works: for in contemplation you serve yourself alone, but in works of charity you serve the many.

To this Christ admonishes us by his whole life and those of all his saints, every one of whom he drove forth into the world to teach the multitude. St. Paul said to Timothy, "Beloved, preach the Word

Theatrics - Page 490, Mystical works of Meister Eckhart

The basis for a man's essence and ground being wholly good, and from which a man's works derive their goodness, is that a man's whole mind shall be entirely turned toward God. Turn all your study to letting God grow great for you, so that all your sincerity and striving is directed toward Him in all that you do or leave undone. In truth, the more you have of this, the better all your works, of whatever kind, will be. Hold fast to God, and He will fasten all goodness to you. If you seek God, you will find God and all goodness.

Theatrics - Page 493, Mystical works of Meister Eckhart

That man finds greater praise before God, for he takes all things as divine, and as greater than they are in themselves. Indeed, this requires zeal and love and a clear perception of the interior life, and a watchful, true, wise, and real knowledge of what the mind is occupied with among things and people. This cannot be learned by running away, by fleeing into the desert away from outward things; a man must learn to acquire an inward desert, wherever and with whomever he is. He must learn to break through things and seize his God in them, and to make His image grow in himself in essential wise. It is just like learning to write: truly, if a man is to acquire this art, he must apply himself and practice hard, however heavy and bitter a task it seems to him, and however impossible. If he is prepared to practice diligently and often, he will learn and master the art

Theatrics - Page 497, Mystical works of Meister Eckhart

You should also know that the good will cannot miss God. But the mind's perceptive faculty sometimes misses Him, and often thinks God has gone away. What should you do then? Do exactly the same as if you were in the greatest comfort; learn to do the same when you are in the greatest distress, and behave just as you behaved then. No counsel is so good for finding God as to seek where you left Him; and if you now do, while you miss Him, just as you did when you last had Him, then you will find Him. But a good will never loses or misses God at any time. Many people say, 'We have a good will,' but they have not God's will: they want to have their will, or they want to teach our Lord to do such and such. That is not good will. We must seek to find God's own dearest will. God's intent in all things is that we should give up our will

Theatrics – Page 529, Mystical works of Meister Eckhart

Further, I declare, all suffering comes from love and attachment. So if I suffer on account of transitory things, then I and my heart have love and attachment for temporal things, I do not love God with all my heart and do not yet love that which God wishes me to love with Him. Is it any wonder then that God permits me to be rightly afflicted with loss and sorrow?

Theatrics – Page 536, Mystical works of Meister Eckhart

if you would seek and find perfect joy and comfort in God, see to it that you are free of all creatures and of all comfort from creatures; for assuredly, as long as you are or can be comforted by creatures, you will never find true comfort. But when nothing can comfort you but God, then God will comfort you, and with Him and in Him all that is bliss. While what is not God comforts you, you will have no comfort here or hereafter, but when creatures give you no comfort and you have no taste for them, then you will find comfort both here and hereafter.

Theatrics: The Nobleman – Page 560, Mystical works of Meister Eckhart

The third stage is when a man withdraws more and more from his mother and, being further and further from her lap, escapes from care and casts off fear so that, even if he might with impunity do evil and injustice to all, he would have no wish to do so, for he is so bound to God with love in eagerness, until God establishes and leads him in joy, sweetness, and bliss, wherein he cares nothing for whatever is repugnant and alien to God.

The fourth stage is when he grows more and more, and be comes rooted in love and in God, so that he is ready to welcome any trial, temptation, adversity, and suffering willingly, gladly, eagerly, and joyfully.

The fifth stage is when he lives altogether at peace with him self, resting calmly in the richness and abundance of the supreme ineffable wisdom.

The sixth stage is when a man is de-formed and transformed10 by God's eternity, and has attained total forgetfulness of tran sitory, temporal life and is drawn and translated into a divine image, having become the child of God. Beyond this there is no higher stage,11 and there there is eternal rest and bliss, for the final end of the inner man and the new man is eternal life.

Theatrics: The Nobleman – Page 570, Mystical works of Meister Eckhart

'Then I hear that all prayers and good works are wasted because God does not allow Himself to be moved by anyone with such things, and yet it is said that God wants us to pray to Him for everything.'

Now you should mark me well, and understand properly if you can, that God in His first eternal glance (if we can assume that there was a first glance) saw all things as they should occur, and saw in the same glance when and how He would create all creatures and when the Son would become man and suffer; He saw too the least prayer and good work that anyone should do, and saw which prayers and devotion He would and should accede to; He saw that you will call upon Him earnestly tomorrow and pray to Him, but God will not grant your petition and prayer tomorrow, for He has granted it in

On Detachment His eternity, before ever you became a man. But if your prayer is not sincere and in earnest, God will not deny it to you now, for He has denied it to you in His eternity.

And thus God has regarded all things in His first eternal glance, and God performs nothing afresh, for all has been performed in advance. Thus God ever stands in His immovable detachment, and yet the prayers and good works of people are not wasted, for he who does well will be rewarded, and he who does evil will reap accordingly.

Theatrics: The Nobleman – Page 57, Mystical works of Meister Eckhart

That is why detach ment is best, for it purifies the soul, purges the conscience, kindles the heart, awakens the spirit, quickens the desire, makes us know God and, cutting off creatures, unites us with God.

Now take note, all who have good sense! The swiftest steed to bear you to His perfection is suffering, for none will enjoy greater eter nal bliss than those who stand with Christ in the greatest bitterness. Nothing is more gall-bitter than suffering, nothing more honey-sweet than having suffered. Nothing disfigures the body before men like suffering, and nothing beautifies the soul before God like having suffered. The finest foundation on which this perfection can rest is humility. For whatever man's nature creeps here below in the deepest lowliness, that man's spirit will soar aloft to the heights of the God head, for joy brings sorrow and sorrow joy. And so, whoever would attain perfect detachment should strive for perfect humility, and thus he will come to the neighborhood of God.

My experience with Meister Eckhart

I had an internal struggle about whether I should write about Meister Eckard or include another Saint that I had chosen. However, the moment I decided to write about Meister Eckhart, a presence filled the room where I was praying.

The air shifted, and I immediately could feel Jesus move into the room, I looked at Him in surprise. His eyes met mine in the realms of the kingdom, and He said something very unexpected, "My son, sometimes the people most persecuted on earth, those despised by their peers, need to be restored to the place they have in my heart in heaven. It is not a good situation, that these men, who have loved me so much, is so despised on earth."

Meister Eckhart was then introduced to me by Jesus, the man carried a presence of Gods emanating glory shining from his being, I realized this man really knew God and understood parts of God that few have explored.

Meister Eckhart loves the intricacies of the new soul; the birth, being molded from heaven, and placed in the vessel of the old soul, yet vastly different in every way.

This new soul is implanted into the being of man to help us comprehend the new mind of Christ and to understand the divine revelation of God and the spiritual dimension. When the new soul is born in you, the process of divine detachment becomes a reality in your life as you live a life of sanctification, a dying to self.

Detachment is a state of being where the soul no longer yearns for the treasures of earth or physical gratification, but the soul is trained by the divine gaze to change the value system of materiality and desire. Desire can now be attuned to the divine harmony of creation.

Detachment creates a vessel of emptiness that can be filled with the divine essence and is able to handle the presence and power of divinity. Nothing else can fill this place of complete emptiness to overflow of abundance. The place of detachment in the believer becomes a place of rest and surrender.

To practice this art of detachment is then the art of objective observation, cultivating your consciousness and awareness, without judging or overlaying your identity or ideas, and allowing the divine God to be only the initiator and infill the vessel.

At the time of the encounter, I did not know all the details of the life of Meister Eckhart. I was aware of his teachings, I had read some of his works, but the fact that he was branded a heretic, and despised by the church, was not something I had researched or knew much about. As I read about his life, and understood all the details, I realized what Jesus spoke about and that the vessel that God uses is one that is surrendered in heart and mind.

QUESTIONS

1. Which part of his story did you enjoy?

2. Considering his impact on modern society, do you think your thoughts could influence the world of tomorrow?

3. Is there such a thing as Theological innovation?

4. What would the impact be if God gave you an idea for 30 years in the future, today?

5. How do you build a thinking system, and financial system that impacts the 3rd and 4th generation?

6. Can there be generational momentum based on spiritual inheritance?

BONUS CHAPTER
Tekle Haymanot

BONUS CHAPTER - Tekle Haymano

Born:	1215
Died:	1313
Nationality:	Ethiopia
Location:	Debre Libanos, Ethiopia
Outlook:	Ethiopian Orthodox Church
Confessor & Abbot:	Iyasus Mo'a
Interests:	Prayer
Achievements:	Evangelized a whole Ethiopian region
Key Teachings:	Prayer, Fasting
Supernatural miracles:	Levitation

Introduction and Historical context of Ethiopian Christian Culture

We have all read the account in Acts of Philip the Apostle, preaching to the Ethiopian Eunuch. Hence, we believe the church in Ethiopia was one of the first places where the Gospel was preached between 42 AD to 52 AD.

Then the angel of the Lord said to Philip, "Start out and go south to the road that leads down from Jerusalem to Gaza". So he set out and was on his way when he caught sight of an Ethiopian. This man was a eunuch, a high official of the Kandake (Candace) Queen of Ethiopia in charge of all her treasure." (Acts, 8:26-27)

John Van Ruysbroeck also speaks of the "Ethiopians present in Jerusalem" and mentions that they were able to understand the preaching of Apostle Peter in Acts 2:38. Other accounts also include Ethiopian lands as the place where Mathew the Apostle preached the gospel.

In the fourth century, Christianity became widespread in Ethiopia under King Ezana, in the Axumite kingdom. The king sent Frumentius (Syrian Greek) to Alexandria to ask Patriarch St Athanasius to appoint a Bishop to Ethiopia, the Patriarch renamed Frumentius by giving him the name, Selama, and appointed him as the Bishop, to return to King Ezana with his blessing.

The Ethiopian Church believes in one perfectly unified nature of Christ, the complete union of the divine nature and the nature of man. This belief is not shared by the Roman Catholic Church, or the Eastern Orthodox Church and some other denominations of Christianity.

At the council of Chalcedon in 451AD, the disagreement between the two stances on the nature of Christ split the church for the first time; 500 bishops did not want to accept the 2 natures' argument.

The Coptic Orthodox Church of Egypt and the Ethiopian Orthodox Church have always kept close relationships with each other. In 1507 Matheus the Armenian was sent by the Ethiopian king to Portugal to ask for military assistance against the Adal Sultanate.

In 1520 a Portuguese envoy landed in Ethiopia, after convincing Susenyos I to make Catholicism the State Church, the Emperor was faced with revolt by his own people, ceding the throne to his son, whom restored the Ethiopian Orthodox Church as the State Church.

The Ethiopian Orthodox Tewahedo Church was part of the Coptic Orthodox Church of Alexandria in terms of administration and function, from the 4th Century to 1959. Pope Cyril VI allowed the Church to have its patriarch in 1959, Abuna Basilios, although the two churches are still in a close relationship.

The Church has a rich modern history; however, we would like to only focus on the early history of the Ethiopian church due to the scope of the book, many interesting Ethiopian Christian practices still influence the Church at large, and their contribution to Christianity continues to bless the nations.

The Life of Tekle Haymanot

Tekle Haymanot was born on 1215AD, in Zorare, on the eastern edge of Ethiopia. He was the son of an Ethiopian Orthodox Priest, Tsega Zeab, and his mother was Egzi'e Haraya.

As a boy he served in the Church as a deacon, consecrated by Metropolitan Qerelos. When he was older, he was married to the daughter of a community elder, however, his wife died after 3 years of marriage.

While on a hunting trip, Tekle heard the call of God, *"Fear not, my beloved one; as of now thou shalt not be hunter of animals but fisher of souls of many sinners, for I have chosen thee from the womb of thy mother and sanctified thee like Jeremiah the Prophet and John the Baptist. Behold, I have given thee the authority to heal the sick and to drive away evil spirits from all places."*

After this experience, Tekle gave away all his possessions and started his work to preach among the community. He came under persecution by the local chiefs still practicing their traditional beliefs and sought for advice from the church leadership.

Tekle was ordained as a priest by the Egyptian Bishop Cyril, which enabled him to formally minister in the Orthodox Church.

At the age of 30, he started a pilgrimage journey, from Selale to Graya, Katata, Damot, Amhara, ending at the monastery of Iyasus Moa in the middle of Lake Hayq.

He then studied under the abbot for nine years. Iyyasus Mo'a the founder of the monastery at Lake Hayq, the mentor monk also further initiated Tekle into the tradition of the Ethiopian church.

The monastery was intricately linked to the royal court and supported by the king. The finances were used to educate the priests and to translate from the original Egyptian manuscripts, into the native language of Geez.

He then traveled to Axum, and later Debre Damo where abbot Yohanni anointed him into the highest stage of initiation of the Ethiopian Church, which enabled him to consecrate and ordain priests.

Tekle, then returned to the region of his birth, to establish a monastery with his followers, and bring some of the spirit of renewal which existed in the north of the Ethiopian region.

The Monastery of Asbo was established in 1284 and became one of the most important monastic communities in the Church.

Tekle died 29 years after the founding of the first monastery, in 1313. He was buried in the cave where he was originally a hermit.

Miracles of Tekle Haymanot

The stories recorded here are from his "hagiography," these were written as a biography, however, it might be a bit idealized as the precise details and dates were not possible in the context.

African oral tradition is accurate, due to the many memorization techniques that were used to train the storytellers and historians of a tribe. One might think this record was inaccurate, however, the amount of information that needed to be communicated could not be remembered in the normal way. The initiate had to learn the stories by heart, and the oral tradition was strict on details and did not look kindly on exaggeration of the stories. A Western understanding of the history of Africa presumes this oral tradition to be crude, however, the process of transmission, the effort to remember the details is a beautiful tradition of community and remembrance.

The focus on the lesson of the stories has been largely ignored by many scholars in the West, but this has been changing, as modern scholars start to appreciate the value of myth, legends and stories to transmit facts and details of ancient times. Somehow humanity is starting to realize, if we will recover from the amnesia of our origins, it will need to be done, on the wings of the words of our fathers, and the stories told on the lap of our mothers, not just in books filled with dusty pages, but ancient stories that go way beyond our modern understanding.

Priesthood

Then he became a priest and his prayers and fasting increased. He stayed with his father until his mother passed away on the 12th of Mesra. Then his father passed away too. One day while he was practicing his hobby of hunting in the woods, God appeared to him held on the wings of angels saying: "I am your God who protected you since your childhood... Now you hunt people instead of animals. From now your name will be "Takla Hemanoat"." Then the heavenly insight disappeared.

Ketana believes in Christ

The saint heard that in "Ketana" the people worship a tree that is haunted by a devil which they fear. They were also controlled by a group of magicians. So he went there and prayed until the devil cried out: "Send Takla Hemanoat away. He is dangerous". Then the saint asked for the help of the Archangel and hence asked the tree to follow him. Its roots made a sound like thunder while it was moving and a lot of people were afraid and the roots killed a lot on the road. The devil shouted asking the saint why he was torturing him and if it wasn't enough that he left the land of "Talanes"? The saint asked the devil to confess before all the people that he was cheating and to tell them who the real God is, so the devil confessed that Jesus Christ is the real God. The saint started preaching the people and they were all baptized. They were 111,500.

Healing for the Demonized Prince

While the saint was devoted to praying and fasting in the desert, he heard a voice calling him 3 times asking him to go to "Damout" because there are many people there who needed preaching. Saint Takla was asked to build a church under the name of Virgin Mary there. While he was on his way to "Damout", Saint Takla Haymanot was haunted by many devils and he crossed himself to force them away. When he got there, he started breaking all the statues that the people worship. The saint knew that the son of the prince was haunted by a devil; so he prayed for him and the devil got out in the shape of a monkey. The prince believed in Christ and was baptized along with his wife and son.

The king believes in Jesus

Saint Takla was able to cure a lot of diseases and got out devils by praying to God. When king "Montemly" heard that Saint Takla baptized his son, he was very sad and sent his soldiers to the prince to extradite Saint Takla, but the prince refused. So the king sent more soldiers to get the prince and the saint. When they reached the king, they were tortured a lot, but God's angel cured them. Then they were thrown in a cave full of monsters, but again God's angel got them out safely. Then the king himself tried to throw a spear at Saint Takla, but his hand was paralyzed and he cried of pain. The king then ordered the two men to be hanged on two trees. But when the saint was hanged by the neck in the tree, it bent till the saint's feet reached the ground, and there were holy lights from heaven and people saw angels... All this happened till the king at last believed in God and was baptized.

Tekla told to move to Amhara

Then one day Jesus Christ appeared to the saint and told him to go to the land of "Amhara" and stay in its monastery until He talks to him again and told him that Michael the Archangel would be with him. On his way to the land of "Amhara", Saint Takla met a monk and they both went to the monastery on a holy cloud prepared by God till they reached there in two days instead of several months.

Move to the monastery of Saint Stephan's

When the saint was known all over the place, he asked God to protect him from pride, so Michael the Archangel appeared to him and told him to go to the monastery of "Saint Stephans". On the way he saw a deep river that he couldn't cross, so an angel appeared to him and asked him to follow him on the surface of the water. The angel disappeared and the saint appeared as if he was walking on land, until he reached the other side. He lived there in great awe; always praying and fasting.

Monastery at Fakharany

From there Saint Takla Hemanoat got out to the land of the "Fakharany" with the guidance of the angel. He went there to a saint monk called "John" and remained there under his guidance for 12 years in the monastery of "Adgway". The angel appeared to the saint and asked him to go to a cave down the valley. The saint said goodbye to the head monk of the monastery and all the monks went out to see him off. The monks were used to tying whoever gets down with a rope (since the monastery was on top of a hill). While Saint Takla was going down, the rope was cut and the monks were terrified, but they saw six wings getting out from his sides, and carried him until he reached the ground. The monks got back glorifying God for his greatness and for protecting his people.

Telkle visiting the Holy City – Jerusalem

Our saint got down to a big desert, and he found there many saints who were used to fasting for five days and do not eat any food; but they were used to eating from the desert plants and drink from the dew drops on Saturdays and Sundays. He visited many monasteries and churches and he was very keen on visiting Jerusalem, so he went there and saw where Jesus was baptized. Then the angel of God appeared to Saint Takla telling him to go to the land of "El-Sofan" where his grave would be, and there he should build a church bearing his name.

Telkle visiting the holy city, Shwiry, where his leg was broken

He last settled in the land of "Shawiry" where he built his well-known monastery known as "Elbianos". Many people followed him and became Monks. He exerted a lot of effort in praying and fasting and kneeling before God. He even used to pray standing on one foot; the right one, until his leg was broken! His monks took it and covered it. He never got out of his cave, but remained there till his death.

Cultural traditions of the Ethiopian Orthodox Church

I have made a decision that before I write about any church or culture outside of my own experience, I will make an effort to spend time with that community, to learn their ways, to understand their culture, without coming with all my judgements and preconceived ideas.

I thus need to first explain my interaction with the Ethiopian Orthodox Church. I understand we all come to life, with our own baggage and ideas, but at the very least, I want to find the beauty and truth in every culture and find some common ground, before I form my own ideas and express my own thoughts on other people's experience of God. My core belief is this, if they love Jesus, believe in the trinity, and have lives that testify to a relationship with the living God, the rest of the stuff that divides us, is less important, and thus needs less of my attention.

I attended our local Ethiopian Church for several months as I was seeking answers from God and met some amazing people in the process. I spoke to the Priest a few times as I was engaging with them and found that the beauty of the Ethiopian people was also in the way that they worshipped God.

There are a few protocols to follow when wanting to engage with the community. One of the protocols is to wear a white covering cloth, this is called a "Gabi" or "Shamma", when entering the holy sanctuary. Another is to remove your shoes in the church. You are not to bring any food or drink into the church. These protocols were conveyed to me as I was partaking in the services and I felt loved by them allowing me to partake and not require me to know everything that is required.

The church is considered holy. Prayer and chanting are done standing. The service starts at daybreak. Which is about 6am in Africa, however some of the priests and deacons are already at the church praying from between 4am-5am in the morning. Most services last until 11am to 12pm, depending on the time of year, and the specific festivity related to the season.

Some churches provide a prayer staff, or prayer stick, this staff is used to rest the head, or the chin on the stick, and enables elderly members of the community to stand for the hours of chanting required.

The most fascinating part of becoming part of this community was that one needs to be baptized first and receive a new "Holy Spirit" name, or an Ethiopian orthodox name, as part of the church initiation. It reminded me of God saying that He will give me a new name.

Community and hospitality are observed after the service as most Ethiopian churches serve food afterwards prepared by the congregation.

My experience with Tekle Haymot

Tekle has as exceptionally soft nature, like most Ethiopian men, he comes across as quiet, and often stoic in nature, yet under the silence, one sees the typical strength of an African man.

Tekle was not comfortable sharing his thoughts with any outsiders, he felt westerners had long misunderstood their culture and their ways. But love required us to also trust and Takle loved the church.

Slowly the words came from his singing lips, he wanted us to sing together first, to chant the songs of the ancient church, to hear the frequency of my heart before we start speaking about the deeper things, his voice echoed in the realms, he chanted slowly, like a man in the field, hewing his plow fork.

The rhythm of his chanting sounded ancient, songs about the past, songs about God, songs of worship sang in times before we knew God was God, or the earth looked the way it seems now.

The Ethiopian chant, in the heart of the African man, creates many realms and elevates those who would allow it, into the place of ecstatic trance, like steps into the darkness, the chants would lead you deeper into the places of the spirit where you have not been before.

The chant of the church, this is not the Eurocentric chant, this chant was born on the sands of the desert, the sounds of the earth permeate every note. A loneliness sets into the tone, and carries the heart deeper, and slower, lower and lower, into the earth, for "Christ first descended before He Ascended", the path upward is always downward first.

Tekle explained the different times of the day. He showed me the Ethiopian perception on time, this was not just done to be different, the Ethiopian church developed this way of telling time, to help them walk in places of prayer and chanting that other church traditions have simply started ignoring.

The times of the day would allow for different graces which could be accessed easily because the natural way was open. The sounds of the chants, linked to the times of the day, would open frequencies of decree, or frequencies of supplication.

The different liturgies were not just developed on religious patterns, it was developed based on the access and the grace experienced, this was done by trial and error through thousands of years of practice, trying to find the right chant, the right frequency and the right actions.

It is part of the heritage that the Ethiopian Church has brought to this world and it will become more influential in the years to come.

QUESTIONS

1. What part does culture play in your belief system?
2. Should a culture be destroyed when a person becomes a Christian?
3. What will heaven look like when every tribe and language is before God's throne?
4. Should the church and the state be separate and why?
5. What is the purpose of ritual in the Christian tradition?

MYSTICAL FATHERS WORTH READING

1. Padre Pio
2. George Macdonald
3. Henry Suso
4. Dag Hammarskjold
5. George Fox
6. Blaise Pascal
7. Symeon the new Theologian
8. William of St Thierry
9. Ephrem the Syrian
10. Thomas Traherne
11. Ramon Llull
12. Jacopone da Todi
13. Jacob Boehme
14. Francois Fenelon
15. Saint Gregory of Nyssa
16. Saint Nicodemus of the holy mountain
17. Saint Isaac the Syrian
18. Johannes Tauler
19. Pseudo-Dionysius
20. Bonaventure

TRANSLATIONS USED

1) The Little Flowers of St. Francis of Assisi | Translation Dom Roger Huddleston by Heritage Press New York 1930 #ISBN

2) The Spiritual Exercise of St Ignatius of Loyola | Translation by Elder Mullan S.J

   Public Domaine (1994 – E-text)

3) John of Ruysbroeck | Translated by Dom C.A Wynschenk BV 5080J33

4) Byzantine Monastic Foundation documents | Edited by John Thomas and Angela Constantinides Hero by Dumbarton Oaks Trustees of Harvard University 2000

   #ISBN 0-88402-232-3 (Testament of John of Rila)

5) Ascent of Mount Carmel | Translated by E Allison Peers

6) The Complete Mystical works of Meister Eckhart | Translated by Maurice O C Walshe The Crossroad Publishing company 2009 # ISBN 978-0-8245-2517-0

7) The Rule of Saint Benedict | Thomas Merton by Cistercian Publications 2009

   ISBN # 978-0-87907-019-9

8) The Life of our most Holy Father S. Benedict | Gregory the great by Christian Classics Ethereal Library

9) On Loving God – St Bernard of Clairvaux | Emmalon Davis by Christian Classics Ethereal library

10) Introduction to a devout life | St Francis de Sales by Library of spiritual works for English Catholics

11) Treatise on the love of God | Francis de Sales by Library of spiritual works for English Catholics

12) The writings of Saint Patrick | Charles H H Wright DD by Books for the Ages 1997

13) The life and teaching of Saint Seraphim of Sarov | N Puretzki by Gozalov Books 2008

    # ISBN 9789081276528

BIBLIOGRAPHY

1) Mysticism, A study of an Anthology – F.C. Happold 1963 Penguine Books

2) Saint Francis of Assisi: Brother of Creation | Mirabai Starr by Sounds true

3) Apparitions of Modern Saints | Patricia Treece by Servant Publications 2001 - ISBN # 1-596-55-303-3

4) Alpha and Omega | Mathewos T Abera| iUniverse 2012 - ISBN # 978-1-4759-1129-9

5) Saint John of the Cross | Mirabai Starr by Sounds True 2008 - ISBN # 978-1-59179-796-8

6) Introduction to the Devout life | Piers Paul Read by Society for Promoting Christian Knowledge 2017 #ISBN # 978-0-281-07709-0

7) The Edge of Glory prayers in the Celtic tradition | David Adam by Triangle 1985 - ISBN # 0-281-04197-0

8) Introduction to the Ethiopian Orthodox : Tewanhedo Faith| Alemayehu Desta by Author-house publishing. 2012 - ISBN # 978-1-4685-4889-1

9) The life of St Patrick and his place in history | J.B Burt E-artnow 2019 - ISBN # 978-80-273-0341-0

10) Saint Patrick : The man and his works | Thomas O'Loughlin by SPCK 1999 - ISBN # 978-0-281-07213-2

11) Saint Dominic| Bob Lord by Smashwords 2010

12) Christian Mystics | Carl Macolman by Hampton Roads Publishing company 2016 - ISBN # 978-1-57174-730-3

13) The Little Flowers of Saint Francis | Thomas Okey by Dover Publications 2003 - #ISBN-10: 0-486-43186-X

14) Francis of Assisi : The Life and Afterlife of a Medieval saint | Andre Vauchez translated by Michael F Cusato by Yale University press 2009 - #ISBN 978-0-300-17894-4

15) Saint John Van Ruysbroeck, his life and times | W.R W Stephens 1880

16) The big book of Christian Mysticism : The Essential guide to Contemplative Spirituality | Carl McColman by Hampton Roads Publishing Company Inc - #ISBN 978-1-57174-624-5

17) Ascent of Mount Carmel| John of the Cross translated by E Allison Peers by Sublime Books 2014 #ISBN 978-1-63384-503-9

18) Introducing Eastern Orthodox Theology| by Andrew Louth by InterVarsity Press 2013 - ISBN 978-0-8308-9535-9

19) Meditations with Meister Eckhart | Matthew Fox by Bear& Company

20) Meister Eckhart: A mystic warrior of our times | Matthew Fox by New world Library 2014 # ISBN 978-1-60868-265-2

21) Meister Eckhart's Book of Secrets : Meditations on Letting Go and finding true Freedom | Jon M Sweeney by Hampton Roads Publishing company Inc. 2019 - #ISBN 978-1-57174-847-8

22) St Patrick of Ireland : A Biography | Philip Freeman by Simon Schuster 2004 - #ISBN-10: 0-7432-6749-4

23) Saint Patrick | Johnathan Rogers by Thomas Nelson 2010 #ISBN 978-1-59555-305-8

24) The life of St Patrick and his place in History | John B. Bury by Dover Publications 1998 #ISBN 9780-486-144-856

25) Francis of Assisi : A New Biography | Augustine Thompson by Cornell University press.

26) The Spiritual Exercises of Saint Ignatius Loyola | Thomas Corbishley by Dover Publications. 2011 # ISBN 978-048-617-3511

27) Dark Night of the Soul | Translated by David Lewis by Tan Classics 1916 - #ISBN 978-0-89555-230-3

28) The spiritual Exercises of St Ignatius | Louis J Puhl by Better Yourself Books 2017 - #ISBN 978-81-7109-290-1

29) The life of Saint Benedict | Bob Lord by Smashwords

30) St Dominic and the Dominican way | Richard Woors by Dominican University

31) Bernard of Clairvaux | Dennis E Tamburello by Crossroad publishing company - 1953 # ISBN 0-8245-2516-7

32) The Complete works of Meister Eckhart | Translated by Maurice O C Walshe by The crossroad publishing company #ISBN-13: 978-0-8245-2517-0

33) Meister Eckart | Translation by Anne Schindel and Aaron Vanides by Yale University press 2015 # ISBN 978-0-300-20486-5

34) Meister Eckhart on Divine Knowledge | C F Kelley by Yale University press 1977 - # ISBN 0-300-02098-8

35) A Companion to Meister Eckhart | Jeremiah M Hackett by Brill 2013 - #ISBN 978-90-04-23692-9

36) Eager to Love | Richard Rohr by Hodder Stoughton 2014 - # ISBN 978-1473-60402-5

37) Christian Mysticism | William Inge by Perennial Press 2015 - #ISBN 9781518331558

38) Selected Sermons by Meister Eckhart | Elliot Bramham 2018

39) Mysticism: A study in the nature and development of Spiritual Consciousness | Evelyn Underhill by Dover Publications 1930 #ISBN 9780486123707

40) Loving God - The teachings of Bernard of Clairvaux | Ellyn Sanna by Anamchara Book   2011 # ISBN 978-1-933630-10-6

41) Ruysbroeck and the Mystics | Maurice Maeterlinck by Hodder and Stoughton 1884

42) Ruysbroeck | Evelyn Underhill by G Bell and Sons Ltd 1915

43) Philosophy of Mysticism | Richard H. Jones by State University of New York Press 2016 - # ISBN 978-1-4384-6119-9

44) Western Mysticism | Dom Cuthbert Butler by Dover Publications Inc, 1926 - # ISBN 9780486145945

45) The Essential Mystics, Poets, Saints, and Sages | Richard Hooper by Sanctuary Publications 2010 # ISBN 978-1-57174-693-1

IMAGE CREDIT

All Images are Public Domain unless indicated:
https://commons.wikimedia.org/

Saint Seraphim of Sarov By Unknown author - В день памяти преподобного Серафима Саровского (15 января) предлагаем духовные наставления святого., CC BY-SA 4.0, https://commons.wikimedia.org/w/index.php?curid=72618879

Saint Patrick By Nheyob - Own work, CC BY-SA 4.0, https://commons.wikimedia.org/w/index.php?curid=39732088

Icon of Saint Tekle Haymanot of Ethiopia at the Ethiopian Abyssinian Church, Jerusalem By Maor X - Own work, CC BY-SA 4.0, https://commons.wikimedia.org/w/index.php?curid=38407435

ABOUT THE AUTHOR

Kevin Hall is an author, pastor, businessman and father. He loves the local church and to see God move in the nations, he is passionate about Africa, and enjoys special moments with his family in South Africa.

Kevin ministers to people searching for the truth of the Gospel, bringing the focus back to the foundations of the Gospel of Jesus Christ.

Kevin founded various ministries during the past few years and successfully handed those ministries over to continue the work that they have started. Kevin currently pastors One House, a virtual church community. He is also the CEO of Savantage, an international events and consulting company.

Kevin's heart is to bring people into the fullness of what Father has intended them to be. Bringing people into the understanding that a personal vibrant interactive relationship with Jesus is possible

Seraph Creative is a collective of artists, writers, theologians & illustrators who desire to see the body of Christ grow into full maturity, walking in their inheritance as Sons of God on the Earth.

Sign up to our newsletter to know about future exciting releases.

Visit our website:

www.seraphcreative.org

www.ingramcontent.com/pod-product-compliance
Lightning Source LLC
Chambersburg PA
CBHW071615080526
44588CB00010B/1147